HOW
SMART
ARE
ANIMALS?

Harcourt Brace Jovanovich, Publishers

San Diego   New York   London

HOW SMART ARE ANIMALS?

DOROTHY HINSHAW PATENT

6

ACKNOWLEDGMENTS

The author wishes to thank Irene Pepperberg, Ron Schusterman, Bob Gisiner, and Louis Herman for discussing with me their work and the issues in this book. I also thank Carolyn Ristau for her helpful comments on the manuscript.

FRONTISPIECE PHOTO BY WILLIAM MUNOZ

HBJ

Library of Congress Cataloging-in-Publication Data
Patent, Dorothy Hinshaw.
How smart are animals?/by Dorothy Hinshaw Patent.
p.   cm.
Includes bibliographical references.
Summary: Discusses recent research on levels of intelligence in both wild and domestic animals.
ISBN 0-15-236770-5
1. Animal intelligence — Juvenile literature.
[1. Animal intelligence.] I. Title.
QL785.P25   1990
591.5′1 — dc20   89-24581

Designed by Trina Stahl
Printed in the United States of America
First edition
A B C D E

For all the animals that have patiently given of their time
to help us learn something about how their minds work

CONTENTS

Do Animals Think? • What Is Intelligence? • Studying
Animal Thought • Measuring Animal Intelligence •

CONTENTS

CONTENTS

CONTENTS

INTRODUCTION

Writing about animal intelligence isn't easy. The subject is complicated and full of controversy. But it's a fascinating topic, one that can tell us a great deal not only about the inner worlds of animals but also about ourselves. One of the most difficult tasks is *defining* intelligence, for there are many definitions and little agreement about what to include and exclude from the concept. This book takes a broad view of the subject and looks into many kinds of behavior that different people might view as "intelligent."

The first section of the book (chapters One, Two, and Three) deals with general questions, such as defining intelligence and distinguishing between learning and instinct. Can we find a definition of intelligence that is useful? How much of animal behavior is determined by inborn circuits in the nervous system and how much by learning and experience? How do animal brains differ from ours and from one another? How can we determine if an animal solves a problem by thinking? How can we know if another being experiences consciousness in the way humans do?

The second section of the book (chapters Four, Five, and Six) describes experiments and experiences with particular kinds of animals. Birds are the subject of Chapter Four. Birds have been studied intensively for years by psychologists and, more recently, by zoologists interested in animal minds. These studies have revealed some surprising and fascinating facts about these highly successful animals. Chapter Five considers the similarities and differences between wolves and dogs, animals of particular interest to humans. Unfortunately, few experiments have been carried out on these animals, but what we have learned sheds some light on the differences between the intelligence of a wild animal and that of a domesticated animal. Chapter Six tackles the touchy question of intelligence in monkeys and apes. Because these creatures are our closest living relatives, we are especially interested in them and might expect them to come closest to having minds like ours.

The third part of the book (chapters Seven, Eight, and Nine) first deals with the problem of language, then takes up some of the thornier scientific and philosophical issues of exploring animal intelligence. Language is considered by many to be the distinguishing trait of the human race, so intimations that animals might be able to understand and use it are cause for alarm to some people. And since language by definition involves the interaction of individuals, it is an especially difficult subject to investigate with objective scientific methods. It all leads up to the last chapter of the book. How much we can really find out about animal intelligence? How do we get animals to cooperate with researchers so that their abilities can be probed? How does an animal's life style affect its ability to act "intelligently"? Are there any general principles of intelligent behavior that can be applied to all animals? And finally, are there ways in which human intelligence really does differ from that of the other animals with which we share the Earth?

How smart are animals, indeed?

PART 1

INTELLIGENCE, LEARNING, AND THINKING

A girl, a horse, and a dog—three very different creatures, with different kinds of lives and minds. Is it possible to evaluate and compare their mentalities? What kinds of problems are there in measuring intelligence?

— PHOTO BY WILLIAM MUNOZ

1

HOW SMART IS SMART?

The blizzard came on suddenly, with no warning. Eleven-year-old Andrea Anderson was outside near her home when the storm struck. The sixty- to eighty-mile-an-hour winds drove her into a snowdrift, and the snow quickly covered her up to her waist. Unable to get out, she screamed desperately for help. Through the swirling wind, Villa, a year-old Newfoundland dog belonging to Andrea's neighbors, heard her cries. Villa had always been content to stay inside her dog run, but now she leapt over the five-foot fence and rushed to Andrea's side. First she licked the girl, then began circling around her, packing down the snow with her paws. Next,

3

Villa stood still as a statue in front of the girl with her paws on the packed snow. The dog waited until Andrea grabbed her, then strained forward, pulling the girl from the drift. As the storm raged around them, Villa led the way back to Andrea's home.

Villa won the Ken-L Ration Dog Hero of the Year award in 1983 for her bravery, loyalty, and intelligence. Her feat was truly impressive—understanding that Andrea needed help and performing the tasks necessary to save her. We can all admire Villa and envy Andrea for having such a loyal friend. But did Villa's heroic behavior exhibit intelligence? Some scientists would say that, while Villa certainly is a wonderful animal, her behavior was unthinking, perhaps an instinctive holdover from the protective environment of the wolf pack, where the adult animals defend the pups against danger. After all, dogs evolved from wolves, which are highly social animals. They would say that Villa just acted, without really understanding the concept of danger or thinking about what she was doing. Up until the 1960s, this view of animals prevailed among scientists studying animal behavior. But nowadays, a variety of experiments and experiences with different creatures are showing that some animals have impressive mental abilities.

DO ANIMALS THINK?
If dogs might think, what about bees, rats, birds, cats, monkeys, and apes? How well do animals learn? How much of their experiences can they remember? Can they apply what they may have learned to new challenges in their lives?

Are animals aware of the world around them? How might it be possible to learn about and evaluate the intelligence of different animals?

It is easy to confuse trainability with thinking. But just because an animal can learn to perform a trick doesn't mean that it knows what it is doing. In the IQ Zoo in Hotsprings, Arkansas, for example, animals perform some amazing tasks. A cat turns on the lights and then plays the piano, while a duck strums on the guitar with its bill. Parrots ride tiny bicycles and slide around on roller skates. At John F. Kennedy Airport in New York, beagles work for the Food and Drug Administration, sniffing at luggage and signaling when they perceive drugs or illegal foods in the baggage. Dolphins and killer whales at marine parks perform some spectacular feats, and their behavior is often linked into a story line so that it appears they are acting roles, as humans would in a movie or play. These animals may seem to be behaving in an intelligent fashion, but they are just repeating behavior patterns they have been trained to perform for food rewards. The drug-sniffing beagle has no concept of drug illegality, and the duck doesn't understand or appreciate music. They aren't thinking and then deciding what to do.

Studying the intelligence of animals is very tricky. During the nineteenth and early twentieth centuries, people readily attributed human emotions and mental abilities to animals. Even learned scientists had great faith in animal minds—"An animal can think in a human way and can express human ideas in human language," said the respected Swiss psychiatrist Gustav Wolff in the early 1900s.

Wolff's statement was inspired by Clever Hans, a horse

that appeared to show remarkable intelligence. A retired schoolteacher trained Hans as he would a child, with blackboards, flash cards, number boards, and letter cards. After four years of training, Hans was ready to perform in public. When asked to solve a numerical problem, Hans would paw the answer with his hoof. He shook his head "yes" and "no," moved it "up" and "down," and turned it "right" or "left." Hans would show his "knowledge" of colors by picking up a rag of the appropriate shade with his teeth. Many scientists of the time came to watch Hans and tried to figure out how he performed his amazing feats; they went away impressed. Hans appeared to understand human language and to have mastered arithmetic.

Then Oskar Pfungst, a German experimental psychologist, uncovered Hans's secret by using what is now a standard scientific method—the double blind experiment. When the horse was asked a question, no one in his presence knew the answer. Under these conditions, Clever Hans was no longer so "smart"; he couldn't come up with the correct responses. By observing the horse and the audience when the answer was known, Pfungst discovered that Hans was very sensitive to the smallest movements of the people watching. They would lean ever so slightly forward until he had pawed the correct number of times, then relax. He watched for that sign of relief, then stopped pawing. His trainer unknowingly moved his head from side to side or up and down just enough for Hans to take a cue as to what to do. At the end of his investigation, Pfungst was able to prove his point. He stood in front of Hans without asking any question. He nodded his head slightly, and the horse began to tap his hoof. When Pfungst straightened his head, Hans stood at attention.

Ever since the embarrassment of Clever Hans, psychologists have been extremely wary of falling into the same trap. They are ready to call upon the "Clever Hans phenomenon" whenever an animal seems to be exhibiting intelligent behavior. Clever Hans taught psychology some important lessons, but the incident may also have made behavioral scientists too cautious about the mental abilities of animals.

Animals that are easy to train may also be very intelligent. Some of the most trainable creatures, such as dolphins, are also the most likely candidates for genuine animal thinking. But finding ways to get at animals' real mental capacity can be very difficult.

WHAT IS INTELLIGENCE?

We humans recognize a "smart" person when we meet one; we know who is a "brain" and who is not. In school, we take IQ tests, which are supposed to give a numerical measure of our "intelligence." But these days, the whole concept of intelligence is being reevaluated. The older, standard IQ tests measure only a limited range of mental abilities, concentrating on mathematics and language skills. Creativity, which most people would agree is a critical element in the meaningful application of intelligence, has not traditionally been evaluated by such tests, and other important mental skills have also been ignored. But things are changing. Many scientists believe that dozens of different talents are a part of intelligence. In fact, more than a hundred factors of intelligence have been written about in scientific literature. Psychologists are now developing tests that measure intelligence more accurately and more broadly. The SOI (Structure of Intellect) test, for example, evaluates five main factors of intelligence: cognition (comprehension), memory, evaluation (judgment, planning, reasoning, and critical decision making), convergent production (solving problems where answers are known), and divergent production (solving problems creatively). Each of these is broken down further into many subcategories.

But what about animals? We can't hand them a pencil and paper and give them a test, and we can't ask them what they're thinking. We must find other ways of measuring their "smarts." And that's not the only problem. Since the lives of animals are so different from ours, we can't apply human standards to them. We must develop different ideas of what animal intelligence might be.

The concept of intelligence was thought up by humans, and our thinking about it is tied up with our own human system of values. The things that are important to animals can be different from those that matter to humans. When studying animals, we must test them in situations that have meaning for their lives, not ours, and not just look to see how much they resemble us.

STUDYING ANIMAL THOUGHT

Many pitfalls await the scientist trying to interpret animals' behavior and make inferences about their intelligence. One is inconsistency. An animal might breeze through what we consider a difficult learning task and then fail when presented with what seems obvious to us. When an animal can't perform well, we don't know if it really cannot solve the problems put to it or if it just doesn't want to. Sometimes the difficulty lies in the perceptive abilities of the animals. The animal may have the mental ability and the desire to solve the problem but is unable to make the discriminations being asked of it. For example, a researcher using colored objects to compare learning in a cebus monkey and in a rhesus monkey first found that the rhesus scored much better than the cebus. But rhesus monkeys have color vision that is essentially the same as ours, while the cebus's is significantly different. When the design of the experiment was changed and gray objects were substituted for the colored ones, the cebus monkeys actually did a little better than the rhesus.

Scientists studying animals in nature can run into difficulties in interpreting their results if they don't pay very close attention to what they see and hear. C. G. Beer of Rutgers University in New Jersey spent long hours studying laughing gull behavior. Early on, he interpreted what he called the "long call" as a signal that was the same for each bird and that was made on all occasions. But when he recorded a variety of long calls and played them back to the gulls, he noticed that the birds didn't always respond in the same way. There were differences in the calls that were hard for a human researcher to hear. Beer then realized that the long call was actually so individualized that it helped distinguish one bird from another! The more carefully he listened to the calls and watched the gulls' reactions to them, the more complexity and variety he found in both the calls and the responses. From this work Beer concluded: "We may often misunderstand what animals are doing in social interaction because we fail to draw our distinctions where the animals draw theirs."

MEASURING ANIMAL INTELLIGENCE

Keeping all these concerns in mind, we can list some factors of intelligence that might be measurable or observable in animals—speed of learning, complexity of learned tasks, ability to retrieve information from long-term memory, rule learning, decision-making and problem-solving capacity, counting aptitude, understanding of spatial relations, and ability to learn by watching what others do. More advanced signs of intelligence are tool manufacture and use, symbolic communication, and ability to form mental concepts.

With such a list of capabilities that might be involved with intelligence, it seems that scientists should be able to analyze and compare the intelligence of animals. But it's one thing to decide to test intelligence and another to design experiments that will measure it. You may read somewhere that rats, for example, are smarter than pigeons. But finding ways to compare the accomplishments of different species is virtually impossible. Animals are just too varied in their physical makeup and in their life styles. Scientists have found that different kinds of animals learn better under different sorts of conditions, so the same experiment usually can't be used meaningfully on a rat and a pigeon. In addition, some animals have evolved special mental skills to deal with their particular environments. They might appear especially intelligent on one measure of brain power and very dull on another.

Dealing with wild animals presents new problems. Laboratory pigeons and rats have been bred for many generations in captivity. They are used to cages and to humans, and large numbers are easy to acquire. Wild animals may not perform well in the laboratory because they are afraid or because the setting is so strange to them. And because wild animals are often hard to come by, the experimenter must usually work with only a small number of individuals. Variations of "intelligence" from one individual to the next can significantly affect the results. Primates—apes and monkeys—are among the most intelligent animals, and apes seem closer to our idea of "smart" than monkeys. But a bright monkey may score as well on a test as an ape, while a dull one may be outclassed by a rat. For these reasons, behavioral scientists have realized that trying to compare the intelligence of different animals is a very challenging problem.

That doesn't mean, however, that trying to find out how animal minds function is not worth the effort. We can learn a great deal through studying how various kinds of animals solve problems and how they use their mental abilities to survive in their natural environments.

DIFFERENT WORLDS NEED DIFFERENT NERVOUS SYSTEMS

Hundreds of millions of years ago, the ancestors of today's creatures floated, crawled, or swam about in ancient seas. While all living things alive today probably share a common ancestor, the amount of time that has passed since groups diverged is almost beyond our ability to comprehend. Insects and people, for example, share ancestors from perhaps 1,000 million years ago—no wonder we're so different! Even our connections with other vertebrates (animals with backbones)—fishes, amphibians, reptiles, birds, and other mammals—are distant in time. Familiar fish with scales, such as trout and goldfish, have been evolving along their own separate paths for about 400 million years. Both birds and mammals evolved from prehistoric reptiles, yet it was about 200 million years ago when these two evolutionary lines separated.

Because each group of animals has changed and developed over such a long time span, atttempts to learn something about how our own intelligence evolved by looking at these other creatures are bound to run into problems. As the great anatomist Alfred S. Romer put it, "A frog is, in many ways, as far removed structurally from the oldest land vertebrates as is a man." Those structural differences apply to the brain as well as to other parts of the frog's body, and they parallel differences in brain function and behavior that are not visible.

The evolution of the nervous system in animal groups, especially those with intelligent species, shows a consistent trend. The earliest animals were not especially active. Like a sea anemone today, an inactive animal encounters the environment with all parts of its body equally. It needs a nervous system that can keep all sides in touch with its world. Such animals tend to have diffuse nervous systems, nets of interconnected nerves distributed all over the body, without much central control. An animal that moves about, however, encounters its surroundings first with its front end. The front meets the changing environment as the animal travels from place to place. In general, the more active an animal is, the more its sense organs will be concentrated at the front of its body where they can monitor the changing surroundings most effectively. This tendency has led to the development of a recognizable head, where the senses of sight, smell, and usually hearing are located. With the concentration of the sense organs in the head comes the clustering of the nervous system there as well. In other words, active animals tend to have definite brains. This process, called "encephalization," has occurred independently in every branch of evolution leading to intelligent creatures. Octopuses, flying insects, birds, and mammals all have more of their nervous systems concentrated in their heads than do their less active, less intelligent relatives.

KINDS OF BRAINS

The world of the clam, deeply nestled in the dark, moist sand or mud, barely moving, is totally different from that of its cousin the octopus, an active, intellligent hunter in the seas. The nervous systems of these two animals dramatically reflect their divergent life styles. Clams have virtually no head, much less a brain. Instead, six clusters of nerve cells, called ganglia (singular—ganglion) are located in crucial parts of the body, such as along the esophagus and near the muscular foot. The ganglia are connected to one another by nerve cords, but each ganglion carries out its own duties with little central control.

The octopus, on the other hand, has the most highly developed brain of all invertebrate animals (those without backbones). The octopus brain, like that of humans, is a central command center that controls and monitors most of the animal's activities. Not surprisingly, the octopus, with its large brain, is regarded by many scientists as the most intelligent invertebrate animal.

Insects in general show a high degree of encephalization. But even here, there are important differences. The primitive flightless silverfish, for example, has eight separate ganglia in its abdomen and three in the thorax. The highly developed honeybee, on the other hand, has fewer abdominal ganglia, and those in the thorax are fused into one large mass of nerve cells.

The tendency towards encephalization is clear in the vertebrates. In this group of animals the central nervous system originates in the embryo as a hollow "neural tube" that forms along the back. As the embryo continues to develop, the front part of the tube expands and differentiates into three main sections—the forebrain, midbrain, and hindbrain. Meanwhile, the rest of the neural tube becomes the spinal cord. In the less advanced vertebrates, such as fish and amphibians, the brain retains its linear form, even though some parts are bigger than others.

In such animals, the forebrain is associated with the olfactory nerve, which brings the sensations of smell to the brain. The midbrain receives the optic nerve from the eyes. The hindbrain is the center for the motor nerves that control movement. In fishes, the information from the olfactory and optic nerves is sent by the forebrain and midbrain to the hindbrain, where it is all coordinated. But with increasing encephalization comes an important change. Information is sent forward from the hindbrain and midbrain to the forebrain, which has become the integration center in more advanced vertebrates. The forebrain is also believed to be the center for conscious thought. A more encephalized animal shows more conscious control over its behavior and less action that is merely automatic. Learning takes on a greater and greater role in the animal's life.

HUNTER AND HUNTED

Activity isn't the only thing that influences brain size. Life style is also very important. A grazing animal, for example, must be able to find pasture and water and needs to avoid being eaten. And a hunting animal must have ways of bringing down prey or it won't survive at all. A constant "evolutionary race" goes on between hunter and hunted. The prey animals tend to become more intelligent over generations, for smarter individuals are more likely to evade predators and to find food; the animals that survive long enough to reproduce pass on their traits, such as greater intelligence, to their offspring. Likewise, as the prey becomes better able to elude its predators, the predator species must also become brighter. Among predator, as among prey, the more intelligent individuals will be more likely to survive and reproduce.

Studies of ancient fossils bear out this idea. When the skulls of long-dead animals are preserved, we can get an idea of how big their brains were. California psychologist Harry J. Jerison, a scientist who is very interested in the evolution of the brain, compared the brain size of prehistoric mammals with that of mammals alive today. Since the mammalian brain totally fills the braincase, fossil skulls make this comparison easy. Jerison came up with a standard figure of 1.0 for the average brain size of a modern mammal. Since a larger body needs a bigger brain to control it, Jerison included an adjustment for body size in his calculations. Then he measured the brains and bodies of a variety of mammals, both living and extinct, and compared them to the average modern figure of 1.0. Jerison called this ratio of actual to average brain size the "encephalization quotient." A quotient of less than 1.0 means that the animal has a smaller-than-average brain; a quotient of more than 1.0 means that its brain is larger than the average of mammals living today. The earliest plant-eaters (herbivores) he looked at had a very small encephalization quotient of 0.18; meat-eaters (carnivores) living at the same time had a quotient of 0.44. Somewhat later herbivores had a quotient of 0.38, while that of the carnivores was 0.61. Still later, the plant-eaters had reached 0.63, but the meat-eaters remained ahead at 0.76. Modern-day herbivores he examined have an average encephalization quotient of 0.95, while today's carnivores average 1.10.

Jerison's figures tend to support the idea that a smarter animal has a larger brain. Not all experts would agree with this idea. However, if we examine the brain sizes of modern mammals, we do see that those animals generally considered to be especially intelligent have bigger than average brains. Here is a sample listing:

rat	0.4
mouse	0.5
sheep	0.81
horse	0.86
cat	1.00
dog	1.17
fox	1.59
elephant	1.87
rhesus monkey	2.09
chimpanzee	2.49
dolphin	5.31
human	7.44

It certainly seems that smarter animals have bigger brains. The relationship between brain size and feeding habits doesn't always hold up, however. Among bats, those that eat fruit tend to have bigger brains than those that feed on insects. Clearly, there is more to the relationships among brain size, intelligence, and way of life than we now understand.

Young birds like these swan chicks learn to follow their mothers at a critical period of development. They learn how to direct the urge to follow. In what other ways do learning and instinct mesh to further the survival of animals in the wild?

— PHOTO BY JOAN ZYGMUNT

2

LEARNING AND INSTINCT

In the deep, dark heart of the hive, a worker bee discovers the body of her dead sister. She picks up the dead bee in her strong jaws and carries it across several combs filled with grubs and honey until she reaches the narrow hive entrance. She steps out into the bright sunlight and drops her burden over the edge of the entrance platform.

Meanwhile, in a scientific laboratory a few miles away, a rat is gently lifted into a strange box by a researcher. The box is a maze, with partitions blocking areas so that only one route leads from where the rat is deposited to the food box at the other end. The rat has been here before, and it knows what to do. The animal zips through the maze, bending its body this way and that. Within seconds, the rat is chewing on the food pellets that are its reward.

A rat and a bee—one an insect performing its natural behavior at home, the other a mammal conquering a problem set for it by humans in a laboratory—what, if anything, do they have in common? And what does their behavior say about their mental abilities?

INSTINCT VERSUS LEARNING

At first glance, the behavior of the bee looks remarkably intelligent. A dead bee could carry a disease that might spread through the hive, so the body should be removed to maintain colony health. However, it turns out that no thought whatsoever is involved. Dead bees emit an odor that triggers removal behavior by workers. If the chemical oleic acid, which is released by the dead bees' bodies, is dabbed on a small object such as a bit of wood, the object is treated like a dead bee. Even if the acid is daubed on a live bee, it will be dragged from the hive, despite the struggles that show it is very much alive. The worker bee clearly has no concept of what a dead bee is; it behaves like a robot, responding with a particular behavior pattern—removing the object from the hive—to a specific stimulus, the aroma of oleic acid. Taking a dead sister from the hive is an instinctive act. The bee never learned that she should do it; the smell of oleic acid triggered the removal behavior the very first time she smelled it.

The rat in the laboratory, on the other hand, had been through that maze before. The first time, it had no clue about which direction to go to find food; only blind, random stumbling led it eventually to success the first time. But the rat remembered part of the route so that the second time it reached its reward more quickly, and soon it could zip through the maze without hesitation. The rat's conquering of the maze is a good example of learning—in this case, learning within a framework set by humans rather than by nature.

Learning and instinct—how much does each contribute to the ability of animals to survive in their natural environments? Is learning more important to some animals, while others rely on instinct? Scientists today try not to think in terms of learning versus instinct. They realize that animal behavior is a complex blending of these two vital components. And within the last twenty years or so, scientists have finally begun to see how these two potent forces interact in determining the behavior of animals.

THE REIGN OF BEHAVIORISM

For much of the twentieth century, animal psychology was "behaviorism." Scientists studied rats in mazes and pigeons pecking at colored squares to get food rewards. Animal intelligence was a measure of how quickly and consistently animals could solve problems posed to them by humans. Behaviorism taught that the animals learned by remembering the motor patterns that brought success. They were thought of as learning machines.

For decades the attitude prevailed that animals were merely complex machines, reacting to the environment in appropriate ways because of the way their brains were "wired." The late Johns Hopkins psychologist J. B. Watson, who coined the term behaviorism, felt that since we could not observe such qualities as feelings, thoughts, and consciousness, even in humans, they were not appropriate subjects for scientific study. Only the observable behavior itself, what animals actually do under different conditions, should be explored by psychology. According to Watson, "Psychology must discard all references to consciousness." The goal of behaviorism was to make psychology a totally objective science, to bring to it the precision of physics or chemistry.

The influential Harvard psychologist B. F. Skinner, perhaps the best known behaviorist pioneer, looks upon an animal's brain as a "black box," which is unknowable. He sees no point in speculating what an animal might be "thinking" or "feeling." What's important to Skinner and other behaviorists is how the animal reacts to stimuli from the outside, not what goes on inside the "black box" that leads to the behavior. In its most extreme form, behaviorism dismisses the very idea that animals might have mental experiences.

KINDS OF LEARNING

Most behavioral science research has studied a few basic forms of learning that are easy to approach using experimental methods. The first is called "habituation." In habituation, an organism learns to ignore a stimulus when it has no positive or negative consequences. For example, when a rat hears a bell, it will pay attention the first time. But if the bell rings over and over and nothing else happens, the rat will come to ignore it.

"Classical conditioning" is the "Pavlov's dog" type of learning. For example, a bell is rung, and then a dog is presented with food. The presence of the food makes the dog salivate. After the sequence is repeated a number of times, the dog will salivate just upon hearing the bell, even if no food appears.

Trial-and-error learning is called "operant conditioning" by behaviorists. Here, the animal learns to expect a reward or a punishment depending on its behavior. A pigeon may be presented with two keys, one red and one green. When it pecks at the green key, it gets food. Nothing happens when it chooses red. Soon the bird increases its pecking at the green key. Punishments such as electric shocks are often used in such experiments. A bell may be rung, for example. If the rat doesn't move, it will get a shock. The rat quickly learns to move quickly when it hears the bell. Classical and operant conditioning are also called "associative learning," because the animal is learning to associate a stimulus with an expected outcome.

"Unlearning" is also of interest to behavioral scientists. They want to know how long it takes an animal to stop responding to a stimulus when the reward or punishment is no longer given. Such a decline in response is called "extinction."

These experiments explore a form of learning called "stimulus-response" (abbreviated as S-R) learning. The successful animal learned that by making a certain response to a particular stimulus, it would either be rewarded or be able to avoid punishment, depending on the experimental design. Behaviorists believed that S-R models could explain all kinds of learning, despite a scattering of experimental results that couldn't be easily explained by this model. They felt that, underneath, all animals were virtually identical. As Skinner put it: "Pigeon, rat, monkey, which is which? It doesn't matter . . . once you have allowed for differences in the ways in which they make contact with the environment and in the ways in which they act upon the environment, what remains of their behavior shows astonishingly similar properties."

ANIMALS AT HOME

While the American behaviorists were brushing off the differences among animals as unimportant, European biologists were becoming interested in studying the behavior of different animals in natural settings. From their work came an exciting new science of animal behavior called "ethology." The Dutch zoologist Niko Tinbergen investigated stickleback fish, wasps, and herring gulls, while in Austria Konrad Lorenz studied the behavior of many animals, including ducks and geese. Another Austrian, Karl von Frisch, concentrated his efforts on learning everything he could about how honeybees find food. While psychologists were running rats through mazes in laboratories, the ethologists were studying the natural behavior of animals. They wanted to understand how animals were adapted to their lives in the wild, not how creatures could solve problems invented for them by humans. The world recognized their achievements in 1973 by awarding them the Nobel Prize.

Ethology originated by studying the instincts—inborn patterns of behavior—of animals. Like behaviorists, ethologists developed their own vocabulary to describe what they found. The term "sign stimulus" was applied to a cue in the environment that an animal recognized instinctively. For example, a herring gull chick pecks at a red spot on its parent's bill to get fed. It will peck at any red spot it is presented with, even if nothing resembling a parent bird or even a bill is present.

"Imprinting" is a specialized form of learning studied by ethologists. When a duckling hatches from its egg, it responds innately—that is, instinctively—to its mother's call and follows her. If an experimenter presents a newly hatched chick with a moving object that bears no resemblance to the parent, the chick will become "imprinted" on and follow that object and regard it as a parent. If the object makes the same call as the mother, the following response will be stronger. While a duckling will follow whatever it sees moving if it has no choice, it will select the most "ducklike" object if it can choose, say, between a human and a goose. The period of time during which a duckling will follow a moving object and become "attached" to it is limited to about a day after hatching. From that time on, it will follow the object on which it is imprinted. A duckling that has imprinted on humans, for example, won't know what to do if it sees an adult duck.

In order to imprint, the duckling must actively follow. If it is merely carried, even behind its own mother, it will not learn to follow. Inappropriate imprinting can have some strange consequences. Konrad Lorenz had several geese that were imprinted on him. Not only did they follow him as chicks, but they also treated him as a goose of the opposite sex when they matured and performed mating displays toward him.

The early ethologists discovered that animals combine learning and instinct to organize their behavior. The tendency to follow an object that calls to it is inborn in the duckling, but it learns the characteristics of that object during its first few hours of life. Hunting animals such as weasels are born with the motor patterns that make up prey capture. They chase moving objects, and they jump on them and bite, for example. But they must learn how to put these components together into effective hunting behavior. If a young weasel is raised in a cage and never given the opportunity to romp and play with other young weasels, it won't be able to hunt successfully as an adult. It may chase a mouse and then bite at its rear end rather than at its neck, for example.

PROBLEMS WITH LEARNING

Behaviorists thought that the behavior of animals could be easily molded and shaped by reward and punishment. They believed that they could combine any stimulus with any response in their laboratory experiments and get the animals conditioned. Ethologists, on the other hand, saw that animals had some preprogrammed behavior patterns. Their experiments showed that animals have predispositions to learn some things very easily.

By 1970, it became apparent that behaviorists had been naive in thinking that an animal's behavior was shaped totally by experience. Some stimulus-response associations could not be taught after all. A rat could correctly associate an odor with a food that made it sick, but it couldn't recognize such a food by its appearance or by an associated sound. In contrast, quail were able to recognize dangerous foods by their color but not through odor or sound.

Learning experiments also began to show similar results. Pigeons readily peck for a food reward but have a very hard time learning to hop onto a treadle to get fed. Treadle-hopping to avoid shocks, however, is easy for them while pecking to avoid shocks is something they can't learn. Rats could learn that pressing a bar brought food but not that doing so could allow them to keep from being shocked. They learned to jump to avoid a shock but not to jump to obtain food.

These experiments show that some learning comes easily to animals while other things are difficult or even impossible for them to learn. These results can be understood by looking at how animals live in nature. Birds use sight to recognize food while rats rely more on odor. The connection between sight and feeding in birds and odor and food in rats is so strong that it affects their ability to learn. Both animals naturally move to avoid danger. They appear unable to learn to escape from unpleasant stimuli by other means. With these findings, scientists began to see that instinct and learning are intertwined in helping an animal survive in its world and that such a connection makes sense. The duckling in nature will be exposed to its mother making her normal call. Encoding all the characteristics of the parent bird in the duckling's brain would be very difficult. But since the mother will be the only object present at the nest to make the appropriate call, the young bird will be assured, under natural conditions, of following the right object, its mother. By having an inborn tendency to respond to the cues it will normally encounter in nature, an animal can use the general learning process to adapt quickly to its environment.

LIFE STYLES AND LEARNING

We now know that animals in general are likely to learn one kind of task more easily than another, depending on their natural history. Earthworms, for example, can sense vibrations in the soil. They are, however, incapable of learning to associate vibrations with an electric shock. But earthworms can learn other things. They know how to stay away from heat and dryness and how to find the cool moisture they need to survive. So it shouldn't be surprising that earthworms can learn to avoid a particular taste if it indicates a hot, dry place or to choose it if it means the opportunity to get to a cool, damp, dark spot.

Scientists studying a variety of birds that feed on nectar found that they tend to avoid flowers from which they have recently fed. Such flowers would supply little or no food, and visiting them again would be a waste of valuable time and energy. To see if hummingbirds fit this pattern, eight captured in the wild were tested in a simple experiment. First, the bird was presented with a feeding tray that had an artificial flower on one side. The flower contained a sugar solution on which the bird fed. Then, another flower was added on the other side of the tray. In half the experiments, the new flower had nectar. In the other half, the flower the bird had already emptied was refilled. The birds were tested until they learned to find the nectar right away when the two flowers were present.

The experimenters found what they expected. It was

much easier for the birds to learn to choose the new flower—called "shift learning"—rather than to select the same flower—"stay learning." The fastest stay learning required 282 trials with 130 errors, while the slowest shift learning took 180 trials with 96 errors. Because the birds had a natural tendency to seek food in new flowers, they had difficulty learning that they could get nourishment from a flower they had already emptied.

ROBOTS OR GENIUSES?

It is morning, and the female digger wasp is inspecting the many burrows containing her offspring. Upon entering one burrow, she notes that it contains large, hungry larvae—she will have to bring them plenty of caterpillars to eat today. The eggs in another burrow still haven't hatched—she needn't carry food there yet. Yet another burrow that yesterday had larvae today contains newly formed pupae; she'll have to wall off this one to protect the vulnerable pupae while they go through the final stage of development into adult wasps. Lastly, she enters a burrow with young larvae—these will need only two or three caterpillars today. After she has checked out all her burrows, the female flies off to hunt for her growing family. She will remember which burrows to leave alone and which to stock with appropriate amounts of food.

The wasp's behavior seems remarkable. With a brain only about 1/4,000 the size of a human's, this tiny creature shows what looks like impressive intelligence in visiting all her burrows, assessing the needs of her offspring, and fulfilling those needs. A little experimentation, however, quickly dispels that myth. If the larva in one burrow is switched with the egg in another, the wasp won't notice the switch. She will stock the egg's burrow with fat, juicy caterpillars, even after examining and touching the egg. If a young larva is placed in a burrow that previously contained one ready to pupate, the mother wasp will wall it off, sealing its doom.

Another kind of wasp paralyzes crickets and carries them to the burrow containing its larvae. Before the turn of the century, the French naturalist Jean-Henri Fabre discovered how "mindless" the apparently caring and intelligent behavior of this wasp really was. The wasp always followed a certain routine when she brought food to the burrow. She set the cricket on its back with its antennae just touching the burrow entrance. Then she carefully looked over the tunnel. Fabre moved the cricket a fraction of an inch away while the wasp carried out her inspection. Upon finding the cricket out of position, she would put it back in place and again check over the tunnel. Even after forty repetitions, the wasp reacted like the needle on a scratched record, returning to inspect the tunnel again and again, never able to get on to the next step of carrying the food down to her offspring.

These two kinds of wasps seem dumb to us in their inflexibility. Is this sort of behavior typical of insects, or can such tiny creatures show more adaptability to variations in their environment?

SMALL BUT COMPLEX
Honeybees live in a finely tuned social environment. The queen bee lays eggs in six-sided wax cells located in large,

vertical combs built by sterile female worker bees. Besides building the combs and caring for the queen, the workers tend to the helpless larvae, keep the hive clean, and regulate its temperature. But perhaps the most remarkable behavior of the honeybee focuses on the vital function of food-gathering. Workers called foragers leave the hive every morning in search of food. When a forager finds a good source of nectar, she returns to the hive and performs a dance on the face of a comb that tells the other workers the distance and direction from the hive to the food and indicates the relative abundance of the nectar. After following the forager across the face of the dark comb as she dances, the other workers head from the hive in the appropriate direction and begin to search for the nectar source within a few feet of its location.

Karl von Frisch's work in deciphering the language of the bees eventually led to his receiving a Nobel Prize. It also helped bring the study of ethology to the public eye. The intricate intertwining of instinct with learning revealed by von Frisch and later workers is an exquisite example of nature at its most adaptive and economical.

Worker bees need no training either to carry out their dance or to understand and follow it; they are born with that instinctive knowledge. But with the discovery of each new food source, the worker must learn and remember key information. We know quite a bit about this process. The bee doesn't actually calculate how far the food is. Her body keeps track of how much energy she expends getting there, and this information is transmitted through the complexity and length of her dance. If the food is within a short distance of the hive, she dances in a circular pattern on the comb. Then foragers go out in all directions and search for food nearby. But if the food is farther away, the dance takes on the form of a figure eight. The direction of the source is indicated by the straight line run of the bee between the two loops of the eight. The information is conveyed in symbolic fashion. The angle between the sun and the food source is represented by the angle between vertical—straight up—on the comb and the direction in which the bee makes the straight run. For example, if the food is 30 degrees to the left of the sun as a bee leaves the hive, the dancer will make her straight run 30 degrees to the left of vertical on the comb. The distance to the food is indicated by the number of times the dancer vibrates her abdomen during the straight run. The other foragers crowd around the dancer as she performs, touching her with their antennae so they can sense her direction and the number of times she vibrates. At the same time, they pick up the scent of the food source from her body.

Dancing is definitely hard-wired into the bees' nervous systems. Different strains of honeybees have different "dialects" of the dance. The dance of the Egyptian strain that signifies five yards would signal fifty yards to an Austrian bee. When these two types of bees are artificially mixed in a hive, their communication is confused. The Egyptian workers don't fly far enough when they follow an Austrian dance, and the Austrian workers go much too far after attending an Egyptian dancer.

LEARNING ABOUT FOOD
Honeybees have a remarkable ability to learn the details of their food sources. After landing on a flower only once,

the forager can remember the odor with 90 percent accuracy. After three trips, her accuracy exceeds 98 percent. Bees have a near perfect sense of smell—they can pick out the odor of a learned food source from 700 alternates!

The second thing the bee learns is the color of the flower. Within three trips, she knows the color within 90 percent accuracy; ten trips brings the figure up to 95 percent. Bees can also learn the shape and color pattern of the flowers they visit, but acquiring this knowledge takes longer. By experimenting with differently shaped targets containing feeders, scientists showed that it took five or six visits for a bee to discriminate between a square "flower" and a triangular one.

All this learning, however, takes place within a very rigid sequence of action. For example, the bee learns the color of the flower she is visiting only during the last two seconds before landing. The German scientist Randolf Menzel discovered this interesting fact by changing the colors of an artificial flower as bees approached, landed, fed, and left the feeder. As a matter of fact, if a bee is carried to a feeder and not allowed to land on her own, she will feed normally and circle the feeder as she leaves as if studying it carefully. But when she returns, she won't be able to recognize the feeder and will search all over looking for it.

Bees learn the odor only while they are actually on the flower, whereas they memorize the route from hive to food backwards on their return flight to the hive after feeding. If bees are carried from food to hive, they cannot find their way back again. They don't observe landmarks between hive and food on their flight out, only on the return trip.

Experiments like these show that the intricate behavior

and remarkable learning of bees all occur within a complex framework. Each bit of learning must occur at its proper time within the sequence, as if a set of "on-off" switches within the bee's tiny brain were being tripped in the correct order. Viewed in this way, the honeybee looks like an exquisitely tuned minute robot. But there may be more to bees than that, as the following examples show.

Von Frisch discovered that bees seem to be able to anticipate where food will appear next. His experiments have been repeated by other researchers with the same remarkable results. A food dish is placed a few inches from the hive. After the bees find it, its distance from the hive is increased by 25 percent. At first, the food source is moved only a short distance. But later on, when its last location was, say 200 feet from the hive, it will be moved fifty feet further away. At some point in the experiment, the bees appear to figure out what is going on and will fly out and wait for it there! It's as if they grasped the equation used by the scientists and solved it. Since flowers don't move, it is hard to imagine what adaptive value such behavior could have for the bees.

Bees can also get around other problems in their environment posed by humans. Alfalfa is a common crop grown for its ability to enrich the soil and for its high nutritional value for farm animals. Alfalfa is structured for pollination by bumblebees, which are larger and stronger than honeybees. When a bee enters an alfalfa flower to get nectar, the pollen-covered anthers release like springs and hit the bee, smearing it with pollen. While bumblebees don't mind being pummeled this way, the smaller honeybee avoids such rough treatment. If a honeybee hive is set in a sea of alfalfa, forcing the bees to feed on it, they will react in one of two ways. Either they learn to recognize flowers that have already been tripped and won't give them a thumping, or they develop the habit of chewing their way through the sides of the flowers to get at the nectar and thus avoid being hit. Such behavior looks like real problem-solving.

Honeybees also show a remarkable familiarity with the area around their hives. They may be unthinking in the way they memorize the route to food on their first trip back to the hive. But once they know how to get there, they can find their way even if researchers capture them en route and carry them in a dark box to another site near the hive. When released from the box, the bees fly right to the food. They don't just memorize a string of landmarks leading to each of the patches of flowers they visit; they know how the landmarks relate to one another. These experiments show that honeybees have a mental map of the area immediately surrounding their hive.

LOOKING AHEAD

Most behaviorists didn't believe that animals could think about how to solve a problem ahead of time. They felt animals learned only through conditioning—being presented with stimuli and learning the correct responses. But the ability to imagine how to solve a problem, actually thinking about it, is a very valuable trait that seems more closely related to what we call intelligence than conditioned learning does.

Ironically, it was a University of California behaviorist

named Edward C. Tolman who first showed that perhaps behaviorism didn't have all the answers. Unlike most behaviorists, Tolman felt that what went on in the dark confines of the brain couldn't be ignored. He stated that "behavior reeks of purpose and cognition." Way back in 1948, Tolman performed some unusual experiments using rats in mazes. He released rats into a maze that contained a white box and a black one; both had food. The rats figured out how to get to both boxes and chose them equally. Then Tolman presented the rats with a white and a black box in a different place. When they entered the black box, they received electrical shocks. Upon being returned to the original maze, the animals now avoided the black box. They had combined the information from two separate situations.

Yet another hole was punched in the fabric of behavioral psychology when experiments showed that rats didn't have to explore a maze actively to learn where to find food. Rats carried through a maze and shown which runway had food at the end ran directly there when released on their own. Unlike honeybees, they didn't have to use their own motor apparatus to know which way to go; they were able to transfer to their own muscles information gathered while being passively carried.

WHO NEEDS TO LEARN?
Why do some animals have such detailed instinctive behavior while others learn new things every day? If we compare the life of the solitary wasp with that of the honeybee, we can see why instinct is sometimes better and why learn-

ing often is more appropriate. Solitary wasps are specialists. One kind feeds only on caterpillars while another captures only spiders. Still another hunts for bees, and a different variety paralyzes crickets. The needs of the species are narrow. As long as they can successfully hunt one type of food, they will be able to feed their offspring.

Honeybees, on the other hand, are generalists. Their food changes from day to day, and they must be able to recognize which flowers are providing nectar and pollen at a given time. Generalists have a big advantage over specialists—if for some reason the one food the specialists rely on is in poor supply, they have nowhere to turn for nourishment and will die out in large numbers. A generalist like the honeybee can always switch to a new type of food. But it must expend energy finding out where food is at the time and communicating the information to others in the hive. A generalist can only be successful if its behavior is flexible, if it can change with the time. Because of the need to accommodate change, the generalist has to be able to learn.

This male bluebird is singing to advertise his territory. What can we find out about animal learning by studying how birds learn to sing?

—PHOTO BY JOAN ZYGMUNT

3

THINKING
AND CONSCIOUSNESS

Because animals such as the solitary wasp will "mind-lessly" repeat a particular behavior sequence over and over again and seem unable to go ahead with more appropriate behavior, scientists use them as examples of genetically determined behavior in action. They assume that such animals don't think at all. But is this viewpoint completely justified? In 1976, Donald Griffin of Rockefeller University challenged the prevailing behaviorist views in his book *The Question of Animal Awareness*. Griffin felt it was time to begin to look at what goes on inside the brains of animals. Can they think consciously about events and objects in their environment? Do they have a concept of self? Can they plan their actions ahead of time? Griffin considered these questions as aspects of awareness, but they are also part of what we consider to be intelligence. Since Griffin's book appeared, scientists have begun to tackle problems related to the questions of awareness and intelligence in animals. By 1984, enough interest had been exhibited in finding ways to assess the intelligence of animals that Griffin produced another volume, *Animal Thinking*.

SMALL THOUGHTS FOR SMALL CREATURES

Griffin believes we must not dismiss too easily animals that behave in a largely instinctive fashion. In discussing the stereotyped behavior of solitary wasps, Griffin asks:

> It is worthwhile to examine our train of reasoning with some care. Is it the consistency of the wasp's behavior from one occasion to the next that makes it seem mechanical? If so, we must recognize that the details of the behavior do vary far more than would be likely in a mechanical wasp, if we could build one. Do we deny conscious thinking primarily because the wasp fails to show the sort of insight we expect of ourselves? Is this justified? If a child of, say, six does something foolish when adults can see that he could solve a problem that baffles him, we do not argue that he is not thinking consciously. Could we be committing a comparable fallacy in the case of the wasp?

Griffin points out that there are variations in the behavior of wasps as they dig their nests, although the range of variation is limited. For example, if particles fall into a burrow the wasp is digging, she removes them, but if none fall in, she doesn't carry out the removal motions.

Griffin notes that the situations in which the wasp appears dumb, such as when a researcher moves the cricket prey and the wasp repeats a behavior pattern over and over again, are completely outside the realm of what would normally occur. In natural circumstances, a paralyzed cricket wouldn't move an inch away. So why should the wasp know what to do when a human displaces the cricket?

When we think about our behavior, we are aware of the future consequences of what we do. A parent reading to a two-year-old may hope the child develops a lifelong love of books from the experience. When punishing a child for bad behavior, the parent may realize how important it is for the child to learn to take responsibility for the consequences of his or her own actions. When we are in our twenties, we set up retirement funds that will help support us fifty years later. Does the fact that a digger wasp is not aware of the future offspring for which she is building a nest and providing food mean that she has no thoughts at all while working? Thinking and awareness are not all-or-nothing propositions. The wasp could feel an urge to build her burrow. She might even plan to carry the paralyzed cricket into the darkness of her nest. She could get pleasure from the process of laying her eggs. These kinds of thoughts and feelings are perfectly possible without any realization that her actions will promote the welfare of her offspring.

Griffin believes that people have a psychological reason for insisting that a realization of long-term consequences is necessary for conscious thought. They are more comfortable with the idea that animals are unthinking machines than with the notion that they share with us the capabilities of thought and feeling. The human desire to be unique and special in the universe can impede science today, just as it did when Copernicus insisted that the earth revolved around the sun rather than the other way around.

BEING EFFICIENT GENETICALLY

In our look at imprinting, we discussed briefly how specifying every part of a behavior pattern genetically would be very difficult. For behavior to be completely instinctive, each action must be specified in the genetic code of the animal. For many kinds of behavior, complete genetic programming would require that an enormous amount of detail be "set in stone" within the genetic material. Griffin contends that coding so much detail would not be very biologically advantageous. In the first place, coding the details of behavior would tie up a large amount of DNA. If behavior were so tightly yoked to the genetic material, small mutations—errors in the code—could render the animal helpless. And the rigidity of such behavior would leave no room for adapting to the often unpredictable aspects of life on earth.

Fortunately, there are ways around the problem of coding a large amount of detail, and computer science shows us how. Many computer programs have loops in them that specify a particular block of information. Every time a person using the computer fulfills a specific criterion, the computer "replays" the loop. For example, in a game program, the game may start all over again every time the player's "man" gets hit with a laser beam. Such loops can be ended by just one line in the program, too—after the player has been hit, say, six times, the computer flashes "Game Over" instead of returning to the start. Nervous systems can be programmed in a similar way. There can be behaviorial loops so that every time a particular criterion is met, the animal goes back and starts the same behavior over again. As a result, the entire sequence needn't be specified.

This sort of programming is probably involved in the coding for a spider building its web, for example. Orb web-building spiders don't learn how to create their beautiful, perfect orbs. They are born with the knowledge. If spiderlings are put into narrow glass tubes where they can't build webs for several months, they are able to make perfect ones when they are let out. Building an orb requires several repeated sequences. After an initial Y-shaped framework is built, the spider lays down the radial threads that will support the web spiral. Each radius is built by using the same pattern of behavior, with the front legs helping to measure the angles between the radial threads. After all the radii are in, the spider starts at the center of the web and lays down a spiral thread that holds the web together. Then, starting at the web's periphery, the spider makes the vital sticky spiral that will ensnare its prey. Laying down the spirals involves a repeated series of behavior—the spider lets out silk until it reaches a radius. Then it tacks down the spiral thread to the radius, lets out more silk until it reaches the next radius, and so forth. The details differ between the temporary spiral and the sticky one, but each sequence could be encoded as a behavioral loop or series of loops. In this way, a complicated bit of construction could actually be broken down into a series of repeated steps.

But the spider isn't a complete robot as it builds its

web. If a radius is burned out by a curious human right after the spider lays it down, the animal will replace it right away. Every time the person burns it out, the spider will continue to replace the missing thread for more than twenty repetitions. Then it will "give up" and continue on with web building, putting in the temporary spiral even though one radius is not there. It doesn't get "stuck" the way the solitary wasp does.

MATCHING PATTERNS

Griffin is joined by H. L. Roitblat from the University of Hawaii in believing that instead of having the details of behavior coded into the nervous system, the brain might rather contain "templates," less precise programming of a pattern that the animal tries to match in some way. Brain templates would require less detailed genetic coding than would programming the nervous system with the details of each motor action involved in a behavior such as constructing a nest. They would also allow for some variation in the environment that would be more difficult to accommodate by complete genetic programming.

A good example of such templates could be the songs of birds. When a songbird is young, it can't sing the typical songs of its kind. It can come out with the appropriate notes, but it doesn't sing them in the correct order or for the right length of time. As it grows up, the young bird learns how to put the notes together in the right way so that it sings like other birds of its kind. Scientists have studied in great detail how birds develop their songs. They have learned that a young sparrow, for example, learns the songs of its own kind more easily than do the young of other species. Peter Marler and S. Peters of Rockefeller University in New York City looked carefully at song and swamp sparrows. The swamp sparrow croons a regular, slow trill, while the song sparrow has a more complicated song with both fast and slow sections. Marler and Peters put together recordings of artificial songs, using elements typical of song sparrows but in swamp sparrowlike patterns. They played these and more typical swamp sparrow songs to swamp sparrows while they were young. Months later, when the birds were old enough to sing like adults, they had learned only the swamp sparrow songs, rejecting song sparrow elements even when "disguised" in swamp sparrow patterns. It is as if the birds innately recognized the swamp sparrow elements and were programmed to pick them out among all the notes they heard as they were growing up. In nature, young birds hear the songs of many species besides their own. But by being able to recognize the songs they should learn, they are prevented from making mistakes and learning to sing like an alien species.

Bird song learning is also flexible. If a young sparrow is isolated from all other birds and hears recordings of the songs of other species, it won't learn them. If a young songbird is isolated from its own kind but has a companion of a different species, though, the young bird may learn to sing the foreign song quite well. One scientist placed eggs of captive zebra finches in the nests of Bengalese finches and vice versa. When the birds were tested later, they sang only the songs of their foster fathers. The physical presence of the foster father overcame the genetic leaning toward songs of their own kind.

TEMPLATES FOR CONSTRUCTION

The idea of templates in the brain that animals strive to match is still a vague one. But it can help us to think about how animals with relatively small brains come to produce some amazing constructs. Caddis fly larvae, for example, live in the water. There are many different species, and each makes a protective case around its body that is typical for its kind. The species of larva can be identified just by looking at the case it has made, without seeing the animal itself. Some species use bits of broken shell in case construction, while others carve up leaves from water plants. Still others rely on grains of sand. Somehow, the nervous systems of these creatures are programmed to make the appropriate type of case. Griffin believes that the template theory can help explain how animals like caddis fly larvae succeed.

A neural template could in some way let the larva know what it was trying to produce. Bits of the correct building material would somehow "feel right" when picked up. A piece of the right size and weight could trigger the behavior of gluing it onto the partially constructed case. Finishing the case could be signaled by certain parts of the body touching the inside or the edge. And all along, the larva could be conscious of the cozy protected feel of the case that was the ultimate goal.

Thinking can occur at a number of levels. Because our own thoughts tend to be complicated and to involve an understanding of past, present, and future, we have a hard time imagining the more simple sort of thought that Griffin suggests for animals such as the caddis fly larvae. But the flexibility that such moment-to-moment thinking would inject into patterns of instinctive behavior would be very advantageous to survival in a complex, unpredictable world. Small creatures with limited brain power are certainly successful, as anyone who has gotten down on hands and knees in a meadow knows—there are insects and spiders by the dozens in a few square feet. If they got "stuck" in mindless repeated behavior patterns every time something new and different happened, they wouldn't survive long.

Templates could allow animals to develop the normal behavior of their kind in ways that are adapted to the particular environment where they live without actually learning anything. As Griffin points out, we have no reason to believe that animals like insects and spiders aren't able to perceive what they are doing and to observe the results of their behavior. Before a spider, for example, spins its web, it needs to find a place where there are anchoring points like twigs or leaves the correct distance apart. It could evaluate its choices by a limited thinking process even if it didn't realize that the web was necessary for prey capture.

TEMPLATES AND COMPLEXITY

Neural templates could be useful in aspects of animals' lives that involve unique situations, not just in the more predictable activities like building the kind of home typical of the species or learning its vocalizations. Every time a predator goes out seeking prey, the situation is unique. The same is true for the prey animal that is trying to avoid the predator. Each individual animal has its own levels of speed and strength. The terrain over which a chase will take place is always different, as are the conditions of wind and weather that can affect this vital interaction. When thought of in this way, predator-prey interactions would seem impossible to encode completely in the genetic material. As Griffin puts it, "Conscious thinking about the situation may be the most efficient procedure."

Thinking could deal with the variables of the hunt in a way that instinct never could. It could be combined with inherited templates that help identify predator to prey and vice versa. Animals can have an innate ability to recognize certain enemies. Some birds, for example, are innately afraid of patterns of rings like those of snakes that feed on them. When presented with a wooden rod painted with the right colors of rings, the birds act frightened and give out alarm calls. If the shadow of a hawk passes over the ground, some bird chicks crouch down and remain still. If a hawk model is used, the birds crouch when the model is moved head first. However, if it is moved backward so that the tail leads, the birds are not frightened by it. Anyone with a dog knows that even one that is well fed by its owner will become excited when it smells a mouse hole in a meadow. The scent of potential prey still interests the dog despite thousands of years of domestication.

WHAT IS CONSCIOUSNESS?
"Mind," "consciousness," "awareness"—these are all words with vague meanings. When we talk about humans, they enter the conversation in a natural way. When it comes to animals, however, things change. The strictest behaviorists would say that animals lack any of these traits, how-

ever they are defined. And even most of the more modern cognitive psychologists avoid any reference to animal consciousness. They are much more likely to compare an animal's brain to a computer than to a conscious human mind. The word "cognition" doesn't necessarily mean the same thing as "thought"—that's one reason cognitive psychologists feel comfortable using it. Thought seems to imply consciousness, and the idea of animal consciousness seems to them unscientific or alarming. By saying "cognition" instead of "thinking," they can sidestep emotionally laden questions like "Do animals think?" and "Are animals conscious?"

Consciousness is difficult to define, although most of us believe that we have it. Some psychologists, however, even go as far as to say that consciousness in humans is an illusion—so much thinking, they say, takes place unconsciously that what we call consciousness is really a trivial part of our own being. But while much thinking does take place behind the scenes and while we perform so many familiar actions without thinking, the fact remains that we can focus our attention and thoughts on a desired subject, knowingly think about it, and then deal with it.

Pinning down what consciousness actually is, however, isn't easy. Griffin notes that adaptability of behavior to new and unusual circumstances could require conscious awareness by an animal. He and others also suggest that the ability to plan ahead and to be aware of the consequences of one's behavior are indications of consciousness. Most animal behavior is very much in the here and now, with little or no apparent thought beyond an immediate goal. But planning requires some sense of the continuity of time, of the future. If an animal can make plans, if it can intend ahead of time to reach a certain goal, it might be said to have a mind, to be conscious.

If animals have consciousness, how can we recognize it? What might an animal do that would show us that it is conscious, that it has expectations, thoughts, or insights? A major problem arises here from the very nature of science. If an animal reveals its consciousness by dealing ingeniously with unique and surprising circumstances, science can't evaluate it. Science operates by demonstrating predictable and repeatable outcomes of experiments. If the results aren't repeatable, science by definition cannot accept them. This principle creates a serious problem for scientific investigation of any phenomena involving unique, unpredictable events.

If we set the scientific method aside for the moment, however, we can look for evidence of consciousness in animals. Although it can't be part of their published reports on research, many scientists have noted that experimental animals sometimes act as if they had formed expectations. When a rat, for example, completes running through a maze and heads for its reward, it acts surprised if the food isn't there. Monkeys and apes act the same way. As you read about the behavior of birds, wolves, apes, and other creatures in this book, you will see many examples of animals that appear to expect a particular outcome from their actions.

CONSCIOUSNESS IN THE SEA?
Dolphins are favorite animals, entertaining thousands of people every day in marine parks around the world. They

show their intelligence by their rapid learning, something that can be easily evaluated by science. But they have other traits, too, that may indicate brain power beyond easy learning. Many anecdotes about dolphins recount behavior that appears conscious. By looking at some things dolphins do, we may be able to get a better grasp of what we mean by consciousness.

Playing may at first not seem like intelligent behavior. But a quick look at the animal kingdom will show that only mammals and some birds appear to indulge in play. When young animals play, they are strengthening their muscles and learning how to put pieces of behavior together to form the sequences necessary for fighting, hunting, and escaping from danger. But when adult animals play in an apparent attempt to relieve boredom, play takes on a different significance.

In the wild, dolphins, like other animals, spend most of their time on vital activities such as the search for food. But they may also play. Researchers have watched as dolphins toss bits of seaweed about and catch it in their mouths. Wild dolphins near shore may play on mud banks, rushing toward the shore and sliding up out of the water. The animals repeat the behavior over and over again. Dolphins also ride the bow waves of ships and play about in the wakes made by whales.

In captivity, dolphin play can result in frustration for their keepers. People who work around dolphins know not to leave a tool or another important object where a dolphin can get it. The night watchman at one marine park once made the mistake of leaning over a night-darkened tank and shining his flashlight onto the water, looking for the dolphin. In a moment, the animal appeared and snatched the flashlight from his hand. The man tried to use a net to retrieve his light, but the dolphin kept pushing it just out of reach. When he finally got it back, the flashlight was completely ruined. During visiting hours this same animal would lie in wait with a ball, offering it to passing humans in play, much like a golden retriever would on land.

Dolphins are also very interested in the activities around them. At Marineland of Florida, a pilot whale (actually a kind of dolphin) entertained herself by watching the bottle-nosed dolphins next door perform. As the days went by, she pulled her body farther and farther out of her tank to get a better view. One day, she inched herself up too far and fell over the edge, out of the water. Worried attendants checked her over and were relieved that she hadn't injured herself. They got her back into the water and put up a guard rail so she couldn't fall out again.

Dolphins in marine parks often watch while others train or perform and in several cases have learned an entire performance just by watching. In one case, two dolphins that were trained in completely different routines were mixed up by the trainers. Although their performances were nervous and sloppy, each animal managed to carry out the routine of the other. Only later did the trainers realize their mistake.

Dolphins can also imitate the behavior of other species. One captive bottle-nosed dolphin amused itself by copying the swimming movements of a seal in its tank. Dolphins normally swim by holding their flippers out to the side and moving their bodies up and down in a "dolphin kick." When the dolphin was copying the seal, however, it held its tail still and moved its flippers back and forth like a seal. It also scratched itself with its flippers like a seal, something dolphins don't normally do. This same dolphin also copied the movements of turtles, penguins, and even of a human diver cleaning the tank. It imitated the diver cleaning a tank window, making noises like the air flow valve the diver used and releasing a stream of bubbles like the diver. It used a bit of broken tile to scrape the bottom of the tank, copying the diver using a vacuum hose.

Killer whales are actually large dolphins, and they also show creativity in finding entertainment in the unstimulating world of the oceanarium. At the Vancouver Aquarium in British Columbia, killer whales have taken to taming sea gulls. A whale will hold a bit of fish in its mouth, sticking its head out of the water. The birds have learned that the whales won't hurt them, and they come right up to a whale holding a fish and take it straight from the giant animal's mouth.

There are many other stories of dolphins' creativeness and game-playing. But does this sort of behavior really indicate consciousness? Are there ways of using science to investigate aspects of consciousness?

BEING SELF-AWARE

We humans are very much aware of ourselves as individuals, separate from our environment and from others of our kind. But what about animals? Do they have a concept of their own individuality? Without such an awareness, it seems that many categories of thought would be impossible.

One way to test self-awareness is with mirrors. If a fish or bird is confronted with a mirror, it behaves as if it is seeing another bird or fish in the mirror. Use of mirrors is a classic way to get a male Siamese fighting fish to spread his fins in a glorious display, as if to a rival. Captive birds living alone are sometimes given a mirror as a cage companion. These creatures never figure out that they are merely looking at an image of themselves.

But what about monkeys and apes? Can they realize what the image in a mirror represents? Rhesus monkeys react to the mirror image as if it were another animal. They never seem to realize that they are viewing reflections of themselves. But marmosets, a kind of New World monkey, stopped threatening the mirror image very quickly and then used the mirror to find animals they couldn't otherwise see. After locating the animals by way of the mirror, the monkeys made threats in the direction where the animals actually were.

Chimpanzees seem to understand completely that they are seeing their own image in a mirror. While at Tulane, scientist Gordon G. Gallup, Jr., placed mirrors in cages with chimps, the animals began by the third day to use the mirrors as if they realized they were seeing their own images. For example, they would use the mirror to view parts of their bodies that they otherwise couldn't see.

Gallup and his colleagues then did some interesting experiments. A chimp used to the mirror was anesthetized and marked with red dye on parts of its body it couldn't see without a mirror. Then it was allowed to come to, and its behavior was watched. The chimp would touch the red marks and sniff at its fingers as if puzzled about where the marks came from. When the same experiments were carried out with three different kinds of monkeys that had been exposed to mirrors even longer, however, the monkeys paid no attention to the marks on their bodies. They didn't understand what they were looking at.

Most animals seem not to have this awareness, yet they manage to live very successfully. What survival value could there be for an animal to be conscious of itself? For a social animal, having self-awareness can be tremendously important. It allows the animal to put itself in the place of another and then to predict the other's behavior. Being aware of itself and others as individuals also opens the door to deception, "pretending" things are a certain way in order to fool another. Deception is a powerful tool for highly social animals.

INTELLIGENCE—A REQUIREMENT FOR CHEATING

We don't look very favorably on those who cheat, who try to fool others, but deception is very complex and sophisticated behavior. It requires intelligence. First of all, the deceivers must be aware of themselves as separate from others. They must also know what kind of information their behavior communicates and choose how to behave in order to give the desired impression to others.

Baboons have very complex social behavior. Scientists have observed a variety of incidents indicating that these large monkeys understand how to fool one another. Paul, a young baboon, watched while an adult female dubbed Mel dug in the hard ground for a large piece of edible plant. After Mel had just about gotten it out, Paul looked around and saw that there were no other baboons around. Then he screamed at the top of his lungs as if being attacked. His mother came running and chased Mel away. Paul watched until both the females were out of sight, then walked over and ate the food that Mel had worked so hard to get.

Melton, an adolescent male baboon, had upset a young animal, who screamed for help. The youngster's mother and several other adults came rushing to its aid. Instead of running away or acting submissive, which could have resulted in punishment, Melton stood on his hind legs and searched the horizon as if looking toward a disappearing alien troup of baboons or a retreating predator. The adults stopped in their tracks and joined him in the futile search instead of continuing their chase of Melton.

Chimps are good at fooling one another, too, even succeeding at fooling one another about fooling! One chimp was just about to eat some bananas when another animal came into view. The first chimp walked away from the fruit and sat down a few yards away, gazing about him as if nothing was going on. The second chimp passed by, but then hid behind a tree. When the first animal thought the coast was clear, he returned to eat the bananas. But the second chimp, suspicious that the first was hiding something, then came out from behind the tree and took the food away.

Scientists have experimented on chimp deception, too. G. Woodruff and David Premack of the University of Pennsylvania used a clever method to probe chimps' ability to understand deception. They set up two containers, one of which contained food. Two trainers were also involved.

One trainer was cooperative. If the chimp knew where the food was and showed the trainer, the trainer got the food and shared it with the chimp. The other trainer, however, behaved selfishly. If the chimp indicated to him where there was food, the trainer ate it all himself, giving none to the chimp. Sometimes the trainers gave the information about food to the chimp. The cooperative trainer always gave true information, while the uncooperative one consistently lied. From the start, the chimps interacted appropriately with the cooperative trainer, indicating to him where food was and understanding when he provided the information. After a long time, they also realized how to behave around the other trainer. They began to keep information from him or to give incorrect cues to mislead him. They also learned not to believe what he "told" them about where the food could be found. While these results are interesting, some critics question whether the chimps were actually practicing deception with the trainer who lied.

Anecdotes such as these about dolphins and chimpanzees can give hints about just how aware animals are of themselves and of other things in their environment. But the experiments with mirrors and with deception show that creative researchers can find ways of bringing questions of awareness into the realm of scientific investigation. We can hope that other ingenious experiments will soon tell us more about how aware animals are of themselves, of their relationships with others of their kind, and of the world around them.

PART 2

INTELLIGENCE
IN DIFFERENT ANIMALS

Working with the grey parrot Alex, Irene Pepperberg has shown that birds can be remarkably intelligent animals. What methods can scientists use to discover the brains behind the beaks? What kinds of special intelligence do birds show?

—PHOTO BY WILLIAM BOYLE

4

BIRD BRAINS

It's no compliment to be called a bird brain. Yet birds are among the most successful creatures alive on earth today. Altogether, there are around 8,600 different species of birds. Because of their tremendous variety, it would be a great mistake to lump all birds together as if they resembled one another in their degree of mental functioning. Just as mammals such as a mouse and a chimpanzee are different in their ability to use their brains, so a hummingbird and a crow cannot be equated.

Birds and mammals are, in many ways, very different creatures. Most birds can take off at a moment's notice and wing their way effortlessly to a new location. Almost all mammals, on the other hand, are earthbound. This basic difference can lead to very different ways of dealing with the challenges of life. For instance, birds lay eggs in a nest and must incubate them for weeks before they hatch, while mammals bear live young. On the other hand, birds and mammals have some striking similarities. Both are warm-blooded animals that need plenty of food to fuel their bodies, and both rely most heavily on sight and sound to interact with their environments. Both groups, however, have changed dramatically from their reptile ancestors and have evolved into a bewildering variety of forms suited to a vast array of life styles.

Perhaps we tend to think that birds are not especially bright because the domesticated chicken and turkey can seem quite stupid at times. But birds have roughly the same size brains as mammals of equivalent size, and some birds, such as crows, have especially large brains. Birds may look as if they have small heads, but most of what appears to be a bird's body is actually the feathers that cover it. Even an eagle, which looks like a very big animal with its seven-and-one-half-foot wingspan, weighs only eight to fourteen pounds.

INGENIOUS WAYS TO GET FOOD

Birds often combine instincts with learning to show "intelligent" behavior. Some species of finches that live in the Galapagos Islands use twigs or cactus spines as probes to reach hidden insects. A bird may modify the twig by breaking off parts that stick out or by shortening it. After successfully obtaining food, the bird may hold the twig underfoot while eating and then use it again. Tool use in these birds may be expert, but it appears to be instinctive—all members of the species perform the behavior without having to be taught or to learn from watching other birds. However, other kinds of finches that don't use twigs to get food in the wild can pick up the behavior in captivity after watching the tool-users in nearby cages.

Other birds use tools, too. Some East African vultures throw eggs to break them. When confronted with an ostrich egg, however, one of these birds may pick up a rock in its beak and pound the ostrich egg until it breaks.

The great tit, a common bird in Europe and Asia, can show great ingenuity in finding food. In a laboratory study, these birds quickly learned where to find mealworm grubs hidden in unusual places such as inside plastic cups or under strips of tape. Once the birds figured out where they might find food, each individual bird developed its own way of getting at the insects. While one might peck through a piece of tape, another would pull up the corner and rip it off. The birds watched each other, too, learning from one another where to find food.

Wild great tits made headlines in the 1930s for their cleverness. Back then, milk in glass bottles was left by the milkman on doorsteps early in the morning. The milk wasn't homogenized, so the cream rose to the top of the bottle. At least one tit figured out how to pry off the bottle top to get at the rich cream (certainly an unnatural food!). Scientists then charted the spread of this ingenious behavior throughout most of England, as the tits learned from one another how to get at this abundant new food source.

The crow family, which includes magpies, jays, nutcrackers, and ravens, has a reputation for brains. These birds have the largest cerebral hemispheres—the "thinking" part of the brain—in relation to body size of any bird. Anecdotes about them abound. For example, pairs of magpies work together to steal fish from young bald eagles in Glacier National Park. One magpie pecks at the eagle's tail feathers. When the young bird turns its head to face its tormentor, the other magpie hops in quickly and takes the fish. Hooded crows in Finland figured out how to steal the catch of some ice fishermen. As they were returning to their lines, the amazed fishermen watched while the crows pulled the line out with their beaks as they backed up and then walked forward, pinning the line down with their feet to keep it from slipping. Once they reached the edge of the ice hole, the crows grabbed the line again and pulled more of it out of the water, repeating this series of actions until the fish were within reach.

Jays also take easily to tool use. One scientist watched green jays in Texas pick up small sticks and use them to pry away loose bark and reach the insects underneath. In captivity, a northern jay learned to use short sticks to reach otherwise unavailable food. Five of the other seven jays in the group later used the same method, probably picking it up by watching their cagemate.

In some areas, crows have learned from herring gulls to drop mussels and snails onto rocks to break open the shells. A scientist who studied the birds found that the crows chose large shells and only ones that were heavy enough to contain a live snail or mussel. The birds were patient about it, dropping the snail as many as twenty times before the shell broke. Sometimes they then dipped the broken snails into puddles of fresh water before eating them, perhaps to wash away bits of shell. One enterprising bird took up two snails at once and dropped them both, thus saving itself time and energy.

A BIRD WITH AMAZING MEMORY

If you've ever picnicked or camped in the high western mountains close to the tree line, you've probably met the Clark's nutcracker. This attractive gray bird with striking black and white markings on its wings learns quickly that people who visit its territory probably bring food with them. It is likely to come hopping over to visit soon after humans appear. Because of its mooching habits, it is also called the camp robber.

Fast learning is just one aspect of the intelligence of this amazing bird. In the high mountains, summer is very short, and autumn blends quickly into winter. While food is available, the nutcracker feeds on insects, juniper berries, and seeds. But winter in the mountains offers little to eat, and the nutcracker must store food in order to make it through. During the fall, it hides as many as 33,000 pine seeds in small caches, buried in the ground or in crevices in trees. It must remember for many months where it stored the seeds, even when the coming of snow changes the landscape radically. In order to survive until spring, the bird must retrieve between 1,000 and 2,500 caches.

Caching food allows the Clark's nutcrackers to live year around in a harsh environment, where the ordinary food supply has disappeared by the middle of November. It enables them to breed very early and to feed their offspring nutritious seeds, which otherwise would not be available in the springtime. By hatching early, the young nutcrackers have a long period of time to grow and develop before they must face their own first difficult winter.

Scientists like Alan Kamil at the University of Massachusetts at Amherst have studied the caching behavior of a Clark's nutcracker in the laboratory. One experiment showed how well the bird remembered where it hid its seeds. The researchers put a nutcracker in a room with a sand-covered floor. The room was empty except for a food dish and a water dish on the floor and a few landmarks along the walls such as a door and a sink. Two hundred and ten piñon pine seeds were given to the bird. At first he ate a few seeds. Next he cached the rest, filling up the pouch under his tongue with seeds and then burying them in bunches by jabbing his bill into the sand. He used his beak to swipe over the sand, covering each cache.

After he had hidden or eaten all the seeds, the bird was taken from the room and kept away for thirty-one days. Meanwhile, the researchers removed the seeds from the caches. They noted on a map of the room where the bird had buried seeds. Then they reburied half of them. Leaving half the cache locations empty allowed the scientists to discover if the bird used clues such as smell to find the seeds. The sand covering the cache locations was carefully smoothed over, leaving no visual clues.

Before being returned to the room, the bird was not fed for twenty hours so that he would be hungry. Once set free, the bird poked his beak into the sand at twenty sites in the room. Altogether, the bird probed at eighteen of the twenty-six caches he had deposited. He poked at only two places where he hadn't hidden seeds. Thus, his searching was 90 percent accurate a month after making the caches, despite the fact that he had very few landmarks to help remember the location of the food. When he came across a cache that the experimenters had emptied, the bird often kept poking and swiping at the sand in search of the absent food. He acted as if expecting to find food in each cache.

In the woods, many more landmarks, such as trees and logs, would be available to the Clark's nutcrackers. In the wild, these birds often place small items, such as pebbles and pine cones, on top of caches, probably to serve as landmarks. The animals would have to use such clues early in the season, however, before the ground became covered with snow and before natural forces might move the landmark object. But given such features as trees, logs, and bushes, the nutcrackers would have plenty of clues to use in retrieving their food stores.

Even with abundant landmarks, it is difficult for the human mind to conceive of how the Clark's nutcracker can remember the location of so many caches for so long. Human beings have trouble remembering overnight where they have hidden a few dozen Easter eggs! The nutcracker's success must be based on a combination of special brain capacity for the memory of locations and for learning the intimate details of its own unique environment. In any case, the mental accomplishments of this remarkable bird are very impressive.

MAKING CATEGORIES

Some writers have made much of the idea that the ability to organize information into categories is a distinctly human phenomenon that requires a sophisticated brain. Science writer M. Hunt wrote in the *New York Times Magazine*, "We human beings . . . are concept-making creatures: Unlike any other animal, we have a natural ability to group objects or events together into categories." In another article, in *Self* magazine, the same writer states, "One of the really astounding things the mind does, apparently effortlessly, is group similar things and make a concept of them. This is something that, as far as we know, no animal can do." A textbook for beginning students of cognition says, "One of the most pervasive aspects of human thought is the tendency to divide the world into categories." But what these authors believed was a unique achievement of the human mind is shared by the ordinary laboratory pigeon.

Scientists like R. J. Herrnstein of Harvard University have clearly demonstrated the concept-making ability of pigeons. By carefully designing their experiments, they have ruled out other methods, such as memory, that the pigeons could use to succeed in the tasks set for them. Here is a typical series of experiments that illustrates how scientists can narrow down possible explanations for their findings. In the first experiment, four pigeons were shown a set of eighty photographic slides. Forty had trees in them, forty didn't. The photos were carefully chosen so that all sorts of trees were included—evergreens and leafy trees, bare winter trees and lush summer ones. Sometimes the tree was obvious; other times it merely formed an inconspicuous part of the background. The forty slides without trees were as similar as possible to those with trees, except for that missing element.

The bird being tested had a key in front of it. When a slide including a tree appeared on the screen, the bird might get a food pellet if it pecked the key. No food came if the slide didn't have a tree. The order of the slides was changed with each learning session. By the second session, three of the birds had already figured out they should peck at scenes with trees. The fourth bird choose slides with trees at a significant level on the fifth session.

At this point, the scientists didn't know if the birds were recognizing a category we would call "trees" or whether they were memorizing which slides might bring food and which didn't. The next experiment tested the possibility that the birds were using memory. This time, the scientists made up a set of eighty underwater slides. Forty of them contained fish; the other forty didn't. Many of the non-fish slides showed other living things such as a scuba diver, shrimp, or a sea turtle. The pigeons were divided into two groups. For one group, slides with fish could provide a reward while slides without fish didn't. For the other group, twenty slides with fish and twenty without received rewards, and a different set of twenty with fish and twenty without gave no reward. If the birds were just memorizing the slides, the second group should score as well as the first, but it didn't. The first group learned which slides gave food more than twice as fast as the second group. The first group was using a concept, "fish," to make its choices, while the second was taking advantage of the excellent pigeon memory. (Pigeons can remember how to respond to at least 320 different slides that are unconnected by any human concept and can remember how to respond to each of 160 different slides for at least two years.)

Another scientist explored pigeon mental categories by using a different sort of concept—"white oak leaf." The leaves of the white oak are similar in appearance but vary in the number of lobes and in their shape. In the first study of this series, the birds were shown forty different white oak leaf silhouettes and forty other broad-leafed trees. It didn't take the birds long to solve the problem—after about two sessions, they were choosing the white oak leaves over the others almost perfectly. When forty new oak silhouettes were substituted, they easily recognized them as belonging to the category "white oak leaf."

How many examples of a category must a pigeon see in order to form a generalization? In the next experiment, the scientist showed the birds forty silhouettes of just one white oak leaf and forty of other leaves. They learned the discrimination about twice as fast and immediately recognized new examples. Just seeing one leaf was enough for them to form a concept we would call "white oak leaf."

Now we might wonder whether the birds were learning to recognize the negative examples rather than the positive ones. Another experiment showed that this was not the case. The pigeons were again divided into two groups. One group was trained with forty different white oak leaves and forty non-oak ones. The second group was presented with just one oak and forty other leaves. As before, the birds shown just one oak leaf learned faster than the birds given forty different examples. Then, both groups were given a new set of forty negative slides. Both recognized them right away as slides that wouldn't be rewarded. Even the pigeons that saw only one slide of a white oak leaf and no non-oak leaves were able to tell the difference between twenty different oak leaves and twenty non-oak leaves.

These experiments show beyond a doubt that pigeons are able somehow to form a concept of a category and to recognize what belongs in it and what doesn't. In other experiments, pigeons have recognized slides with people and slides of one particular individual human. They can tell that a stick of celery or a climbing vine is not the same as a tree.

Some careful thinking about life in the wild makes the accomplishments of the pigeons less surprising. Finding food is one of the biggest challenges an animal faces. Imagine a hungry bird looking for morsels of food. It tries a new kind of berry and discovers that it is tasty. If it can immediately recognize that sort of berry the next time it sees it, the bird has a big advantage in getting enough to eat. Even though the silhouettes of the white oak leaf were not edible, they were closely associated with food. Just as the bird would peck at the food itself in nature, it pecked at the key in the laboratory and learned immediately that a white oak leaf represented food.

Since the ability to categorize is easily accomplished by birds, chances are that it will prove to be a characteristic of other animals as well. Interestingly enough, though, while even the bird brain finds no difficulty in this task, no human mind has yet figured out how to program a computer to do it. Even a relatively simple category like "white oak leaf silhouettes" is, so far, too complex for us to program into our most sophisticated machines, for we have no idea how the brain forms a concept or recognizes an object. It is one of the wonders of the mind, not just the human mind, that an organism such as a human child can realize that a delicate, tiny chihuahua and a giant, stocky St. Bernard are both dogs.

TALKING PARROTS
Parrots can be taught to say "Polly want a cracker?" and "Ahoy mate" without knowing what they are "saying." But

people over the years have hoped that birds like parrots and minahs, which are quite intelligent and which are capable of mimicking human speech, could be taught to connect meaning to their word-copying. As far back as the 1940s, scientists tried to get birds to use words as labels for objects and actions. But the attempts always ended in failure. It seemed that the birds couldn't make the connection between word and meaning.

Then studies of the behavior of wild birds gave clues about how they might be taught to speak more readily. Mated pairs of wild parrots are quite vocal, dueting with one another and creating their own unique vocalizations. One scientist in the 1970s used this knowledge to teach parrots how to copy human speech very quickly. Two people talked back and forth with each other. One was the parrot's principal trainer, while the other was the parrot's rival for the trainer's attention. The trainer might say to the other person, "What's your name?" The person would say, "My name is Joan." The trainer would then give the person lots of attention for answering the question. When the parrot mimicked the rival person, it got the attention instead. Using this method, the scientists taught the parrots their parts in a duet in a day or less. In this study, however, the birds weren't expected to connect meaning with what they "said."

Beginning in 1977, Irene M. Pepperberg of Northwestern University began using a similar method to teach an African grey parrot named Alex to use words and to connect meaning to them. Two people interacted to show the parrot how the words were used. But instead of one always taking the role of the "mate" and the other that of the "parrot," the two people exchanged roles so the bird could see that communication goes two ways. In addition, the objects and actions that were taught were ones of interest to the parrot. His reward for using a word correctly was to be allowed to manipulate the object. That way, he could investigate it and make an even closer association of the object with the vocalization that represented it.

Here is an example of an early training session with Alex in which the scientists wanted to improve his pronunciation of the word "pasta." "I" refers to Irene, the principal trainer, "A" to Alex, and "B" to a secondary trainer, Bruce Rosen.

I: Bruce, what's this?
B: Pasta (loudly).
I: Good boy! Here you go. (hands over a piece of pasta)
A: (interrupting) ah-ah.
B: Do you want this, Alex? What is it?
A: Pah-ah.
B: Better . . .
A: Pah-ah.
B: No. Irene, what's this?
I: Pah-ah.
B: Better!
I: Pas-ta. (emphasizing the "s" and "t")
B: That's right, tell me what it is again. (offers pasta)
I: Pasta! (takes pasta) Pasta! (Alex stretches from his
   perch on top of cage, appears to reach for pasta)
A: Pa!
I: Better—what is it?
A: Pah-ah.

I: Better!

A: Pah-ta.

I: Okay, here's the pasta. Good try.

By using this method, Alex has learned a remarkable number of words. By 1988, he could name thirty objects, seven colors, and five shapes. Alex uses language to communicate his wants and needs to his trainers. When he doesn't want to continue a series of experiments, he says, "No," and gets a rest from working. He knows how to use phrases such as "Wanna go X" to indicate a place he likes, such as the back of a chair or his wooden play gym; "Want Y," where "Y" could be a certain food or toy; "Come here;" and "What's this?" to ask for the name of an object. Once a nut was hidden under a metal cup placed on a desk. Alex tried to lift the cup but couldn't manage on his own. He walked over to the edge of the desk and said to Irene Pepperberg, "Go pick up cup." Before then, he had used the phrase, "Go pick up . . ." but not with cup. Dr. Pepperberg obliged and picked up the cup so that Alex could eat the nut. Incidents like this indicate that Alex might have some understanding of how to use language.

Alex's ability to communicate in English has made it possible to explore other mental capabilities as well. Pigeons can recognize items that share traits as belonging to the same class. But can creatures other than humans attach a label to classes of items such as objects of the same color? Can they recognize that the same item may belong to a variety of different classes, such as blue things or square shapes, depending on the trait that defines the category? It seems that at least one animal, the African grey parrot, can.

When Alex is shown an object, he may be asked, "What shape?" or "What color?" His responses on these questions are more than 80 percent correct. He appears to be aware that shape and color are different categories of information. One time he may be shown a red four-cornered piece of wood and asked about color, another time about shape. His answers in both cases are appropriate.

But his ability goes beyond just labeling an object. Alex may be shown three differently shaped objects that are all the same color. When he is asked, "What's same?" he answers, "Color." If he is asked, "What's different?" he will respond, "Shape." The ability to understand that objects share or do not share a particular trait and to identify it is considered to be a difficult mental task. This talent goes beyond the pigeon's recognition of categories because it shows the bird can recognize and label shared abstract traits such as color and shape.

Alex knows a lot about color, shape, and material—metal, wood, and paper. When he is presented with familiar objects, he is right over 80 percent of the time. With unfamiliar objects, 70 percent of his answers are correct. David Premack calls abstract categories such as color and shape "second-order concepts." He considered such abstract thinking beyond the ability of birds. But now we know that the grey parrot at least can use different traits of objects to classify and reclassify them.

CAN BIRDS COUNT?

The idea that animals might be able to count has always fascinated humans. But ever since Clever Hans, scientists have been quite skeptical about any claims of animal counting. Pigeons can recognize sequences, which might be a part of number understanding. For example, if pigeons are trained to peck out a particular sequence of letters such as ABCD on keys to obtain food, they will still peck in the correct order when given only two keys—AB, AC, BD, and so forth. They realize that the A key comes before the others, that the B key is after the A but before the others, and so on.

Some birds can recognize quantities when presented with two groups of items. For example, if ravens or grey parrots are shown a random group of six lumps of plastic clay and another random grouping of six spots, the birds can tell that the two quantities are equal. This type of experiment has been done with a variety of birds with interesting results. While ravens and grey parrots can recognize equal quantities up to eight, pigeons can rarely answer correctly if there are more than five objects. Chickens can only handle two or three.

It may seem from these experiments that birds aren't very good with numbers. But if people are shown groups of objects for a short time—too short for them to actually count them—they score no better than ravens and grey parrots. But matching two quantities is not the same as actually counting. In humans, counting and matching may use different parts of the brain, and counting requires more abstract thinking.

Alex can name quantities of objects up to six. He may be shown, for example, a collection of six pieces of paper or three popsicle sticks. He is then asked, "How many?" Alex answers these sorts of questions correctly almost 79 percent of the time. Many of the responses counted by the researchers as errors were ones in which he just gave the category of object, such as wood, rather than naming a quantity. When asked again, "How many?" he was right 95 percent of the time. Since the objects varied in shape and size, Alex couldn't have been using total quantity of material as a clue to number. Odor was not a factor either, since food items weren't used.

To further test Alex, he was presented with quantities of completely unfamiliar objects such as raisins, plastic hair clips, and antacid tablets. On these tests he was correct 75 percent of the time. Since the objects in that test were all lined up in a row, yet another experiment was tried using items tossed randomly on the surface of a tray. This time, he was right 77 percent of the time.

In yet another trial, Alex was presented with mixed groupings of items—for example, two corks and three keys. He was then asked how many keys there were, or how many corks. In order to answer these questions correctly, Alex had to recognize the name of the object and notice how many there were, ignoring the other objects on the tray. In this short experiment, Alex was correct on seven of the ten questions the first time they were asked. His "wrong" answers were instances in which he didn't answer with a number. Here is a transcript of the first trial of this type, in which Alex gives several different answers, each counted as an incorrect response, before he comes up with the quantity of keys:

Alex was shown a tray with two wooden plant stakes and three keys. The principal investigator, who sat in the corner, didn't know what was on the tray. A = Alex, T = trainer, I = principal investigator.

T: How many key?

A: Wood.

I: Are there any wood?

T: Yes.

I: Try that.

T: Ok, tell me, how many wood?

A: Two.

I: Two?

T: Yes. (Alex is given one stake, which he chews apart. It is replaced and the tray re-presented.)

T: Now, how many key?

A: Key.

T: That's right, keys. How many?

A: Two wood.

T: There are two wood, but you tell me, how many key?

A: Five.

I: Five?

T: OK, Alex, that's the number of toys; you tell me, how many key? [Alex hadn't learned the word toy; the trainer just used the word to somehow indicate that Alex had given the total number of objects.]

A: Three.

I: Three?

T: Good boy! Here's a key.

Alex showed that he could usually answer correctly when asked about the number of objects in a variety of circumstances. But do such responses mean that Alex can count? Not necessarily. Other mechanisms of quantity identification could be responsible rather than counting in the familiar sense. Even though the objects varied in shape,

Alex could still be recognizing a particular quantity rather than actually counting the objects one at a time.

WHAT BIRDS CAN DO

When behaviorism held sway over psychology and ethology was in its early stages, birds were looked upon as very much like robots whose learning could be explained through simple stimulus-response mechanisms. Their songs were thought to be largely inborn, only influenced slightly by learning, and their brains were thought to be incapable of abstract thought. For years, no one tried to study birds in a different way to find out what they could really do. But all that was needed was to use the right methods to discover that these animals have many previously unsuspected abilities. Now that scientists are probing more and more intently into the brains of birds, further surprises could well be in store.

Dogs have been bred for thousands of years
to be helpers to humans, and sheepdogs are
among the most valuable and intelligent of
these. How have dogs changed from their
wolf ancestors to make this possible? How
do different kinds of dogs demonstrate their
intelligence?

—PHOTO BY N. A. LYON

5

THE WOLF
AND THE DOG

The old buck fled through the sparse trees along the edge of the meadow, two wolves hard at his heels. Just as he began to pull away from his tiring pursuers, another wolf sprang out from behind a tree and took up the chase. It was too much for the winded deer. As his exhausted body forced him to slow down, the wolf closed in for the kill. Now there would be enough food for the whole pack, including the hungry pups waiting back at the den.

Wolves are intelligent animals. They have to be—their cooperative hunting life style demands the ability to communicate, cooperate, and plan, all important aspects of intelligence. In many ways, the wolf in the Northern Hemisphere filled the same evolutionary niche occupied by the evolving ancestors of modern humans in Africa. Perhaps by looking at wolves, we can understand a little about the origins of our own well-tuned brains. Knowing something about wolves can also help us see in a new and revealing way the mind of our most helpful animal companion, the dog.

Wolves normally live in family groups called packs. A pack usually consists of a pair of wolves, their pups of the year, and their offspring from previous years. Often, a wolf that is reaching sexual maturity leaves, and a lone wolf may join an established pack. For these reasons, all the wolves in a pack are not necessarily related.

Social relationships within the group are of vital importance. Each animal has its proper place in the pack. The breeding pair, called the alpha male and the alpha female, are treated with great respect by the other wolves. Any animal above a particular wolf in the pecking order is said to be "dominant" to it, while that same animal is dominant to individuals lower down. When approaching a dominant animal, a wolf keeps its tail down, ears back, and head low. The dominant animal walks with stiff legs and keeps its head and tail held high. Wolves in the pack interact often with one another, and their communication can be quite subtle. The complex social interactions of the pack require great sensitivity and alertness on the part of its members.

The whole pack cooperates in caring for the pups, usually produced by the alpha pair. Upon returning to the pups after a hunt, the adults regurgitate meat for the pups to eat. Sometimes, a pack member will "baby-sit" for the youngsters while the alpha female joins the hunting party.

Before the hunt, the wolves all gather and interact, greeting one another and often howling together. This behavior probably helps them act as a coordinated team while going after game.

WOLVES AND HUMANS

The life of the wolf is similar in many key ways to that of human hunting tribes. Both require cooperation in the hunt and a social environment for raising offspring. Both spend about the same proportion of their lifetimes as young, dependent members of the group. In addition, hunting species have spare time to spend in social activities after a kill is made, since a big kill may feed the group for an extended period of time.

Hunting species also require a home base where the nonhunting members of the group can live while the others are out obtaining food. Human hunters have a village or campsite, while wolves use the den or rendezvous spot. When wolf pups are young, they stay secluded in an earthen den, coming out only when at least one adult is around to protect them. When older, the pups are left at a rendezvous site to which the pack returns after the hunt.

Some scientists pondering the unique intelligence of humans have wondered if social living may have been the key factor that stimulated the development of our special mentality. They feel that the mental flexibility necessary to deal with social interactions could have been the starting point for a generally more adaptable mind. Certainly many intelligent animals—wolves, dolphins, chimpanzees, and elephants, for example—are also highly social.

How smart are wolves? Observing wolves in the wild is very difficult because of their mobility. But what is known about their lives indicates that they know how to use their brains. Hunting requires mental traits that have intelligent elements. Hunters must be persistent in searching for prey, even when they can't see or smell it; persistence is important in solving any sort of difficult problem. The wolf hunt also shows elements of planning. The animals sometimes chase their prey in relays, fresh wolves replacing those that have tired. Before a rush against prey, some individuals will take up positions blocking possible escape routes.

Wolves often encircle their prey and carry out a coordinated stalk, slowly tightening the circle, leaving no way of escape. One wolf often grabs the nose of a large prey animal, such as a moose, with its jaws. A hold like that would be useless for a single hunter, but it helps slow down the prey when a group is attacking. The wolf with the nose hold needs to be aware that its companions will use deadlier methods while it hangs on.

Wolves also can figure out when the chase is hopeless. They often test a herd by running it for a distance, then quit if no individual seems slower or weaker than the others. All these aspects of hunting behavior require awareness of the situation, ways of planning ahead, and means of communicating among members of the pack.

Wolves have a very clear understanding of the geographical details of their territory, which can be very large. While wolves generally follow game trails and roads when on the move, they will also take shortcuts to get to their destination more quickly. They may depart from the trail while following prey to go to the top of a ridge, where they can view what lies ahead.

Such a mental representation of their surroundings indicates a sophisticated level of brain function. The term "cognitive map" is used to refer to these internal versions of an animal's environment. It was originally used only to refer to a knowledge of terrain thorough enough to enable an animal to take new routes from one place to another. But now its meaning has been broadened to include the ability to plan actions of other types, in the belief that the two abilities are related.

Some scientists think that cognitive maps could provide the basis for human intelligence and for the development of language. Their argument goes as follows: Hunting large animals required human ancestors to be able to travel far in their search for food and to learn the geographical details of a large area, stretching the mental limits of the primate brain. Without natural weapons like powerful jaws and teeth, they had to develop and coordinate the use of weapons like axes and spears. This process required more complex communication than among foragers that gathered food individually. While many animals recognize individuals and key locations by smell, humans can't. So our ancestors, needing a way to label individuals and locations, began to use sounds for such identification. These sounds ultimately became words. And the ability of the brain to form complex cognitive maps could have allowed for the development of true language using those words as a starting point.

But if cognitive maps indicate such mental potential, how are we to regard the tiny honeybee, which can recognize landmarks near its hive and fly straight to a food source even when moved off the track? The bee certainly behaves as if it had a cognitive map, yet its intelligence is of a limited sort. Perhaps the way the bee recognizes its surroundings and locates home is different in some fundamental way from the methods used by mammalian hunters.

COMPARING WOLVES AND DOGS

While directly studying the intelligence of wolves in the wild is impractical, captive animals provide a source of information about the wolf's ability to think, plan, and form mental images. Harry Frank of the University of Michigan and his colleagues used four captive wolf pups in some interesting experiments. One set of studies involved puzzle boxes that had to be solved in order to get food. The first test was relatively easy. The food dish was placed inside an open-ended box that was covered by wire mesh. Two wooden blocks were behind the dish so that a quarter of the dish stuck out from the opening. All the animal had to do was to pull the dish out with a paw to get at the food. All four pups were successful.

On the second day, the wolves were given two tests. In the first, one of the blocks was turned sideways so that the front of the food dish was about even with the front of the box. Three of the pups figured out how to pull out the dish this time. The other test was much trickier. The food was hidden behind a swinging gate. When the wolf pulled at the edge of the gate, the food dish swung out lazy-Susan style. Again, three of the pups solved the puzzle. The third day, just one block was put behind the dish inside the box and a wooden dowel was attached to the front of the dish by a rope. The wolf had to pull on the dowel to remove the dish from the box. The animals were given two trials. The first time, all four pups solved the puzzle. The second time, three did.

The dish was moved farther back in the box on the fourth day so that the pup had to pull the dowel farther to get the food. Again, three pups were successful. On the fifth and last day, the animals were presented with two new puzzles. In the first, the dish was inside a box turned against the wall. The box had to be pulled away from the wall to get at the food; three wolves succeeded here. The most difficult puzzle was saved for last. The dish was inside the box, but no string was attached. Instead, a plunger at the back of the box could be pressed to push the dish out. Only one wolf solved that problem.

Perhaps the most interesting thing about these experiments is the way the wolf pups solved the problems. In several cases, the wolves came up with the correct solution right off the bat, with no trial-and-error attempts. And once a wolf had figured out a string-and-dowel problem, it solved each variation that came up, indicating that the animals understood the basic principle of pulling on the dowel to get the food.

By studying the problems first just by looking at the setup and then successfully carrying out the correct manipulations, the wolves indicated that they were probably visualizing the solution first and then carrying it out. Psychologists regard this ability to visualize solutions as an early step in true representational thought. A lot of mental sophistication went into solving these problems by the wolf pups. They combined their awareness of hunger with past experiences in obtaining food and with an understanding of the relationships of physical objects. They understood how their actions could affect their environment to accomplish important goals like obtaining food.

Harry Frank also tested four dog puppies in the same

experiments. The dogs did very poorly compared to the wolves. Wolves are the major ancestor of the dog (the jackal may be another), but dogs have been selected by humans for at least 10,000 years for traits that make them good coworkers and companions for people. While wolves and dogs have much in common, the basic nature of the dog differs greatly from that of the wolf because of its history. The feeding-dish experiments show this difference clearly. The wolf pups studied the problems and solved them on their own. The dog puppies, on the other hand, were likely to be curious until they realized that the food wouldn't be easy to get. Then they would go over to the human investigator and beg. When that didn't work, the pup would just give up and wait until the two-minute time for the experiment was over. Then the experimenter would get the food and show the pup how to solve the puzzle.

The results of these experiments might at first make dogs look dumb compared to the wolves. Only one dog solved the problem on the third day, and two did so on the fourth. No dog solved either puzzle on the fifth day. But the dogs really weren't being stupid—they were just being dogs. One trait humans have selected in dogs is attentiveness toward and dependence on humans. No wonder the dogs exerted little mental effort and expected the human to get the food for them!

HOW SMART ARE DOGS?
People are very divided on the subject of canine intelligence. To some, the dog is a most intelligent animal, while others view it as being quite stupid. Such evaluations are subjective and depend more on personal experience with one or a few animals than on actual canine brain power.

Dogs have been bred to perform many sorts of tasks over the thousands of years they have worked with humankind. Each task requires a different sort of intelligence and personality. A breed such as the Great Pyrenees, which is left out to guard flocks of sheep, needs to be independent from humans and able to make decisions on its own. These dogs are often difficult to train because of their independent spirit. At a dog show, you are unlikely to see a Great Pyrenees in the obedience ring.

A sheep-herding dog such as a Border collie, on the other hand, must be very obedient and sensitive to the split-second commands of its owner. A hunting dog like a Labrador or a golden retriever must be obedient enough to pick up a tempting dead bird gently in its mouth and return the bird to its master instead of running off and eating it. Such breeds are very trainable, learning a great variety of signals that the trainer uses to guide the dog in its work.

The relationship of dog and human is so close that it is hard to evaluate dog intelligence objectively. Because of this intimate relationship, much probably depends on expectation. As with human children, dogs are likely to respond to what a person expects from them. If the expectations are low, the dog isn't likely to show much in the way of brains. However, if a person working with a dog thinks it can perform well, chances are he or she will get more from the animal.

Sheep-herding dogs are among the most remarkable animal helpers. Without their dogs, shepherds would not be able to perform their work. Sheep dog behavior is a fascinating blend of instinct derived from wolf-hunting behavior and of training, made possible by the dog's desire to please its human master. One important task of a sheep dog is to watch for sheep that stray from the flock. Sheep dogs go after such sheep, often without receiving a command to do so. This attention to the stray animal probably derives from the wolf's need to watch for potential prey that don't stick with the herd. Sheep dogs are also especially good at splitting one animal off from the flock, another remnant of the hunter's habit of isolating one prey animal from the group.

Like wolves, sheep dogs are able to range over large territories, find animals, and return home by the most convenient route. They are capable of forming complex cognitive maps. A shepherd may send his dogs off to collect sheep that are a few miles away, knowing his dogs will find the sheep and bring them in before the end of the day without getting lost.

Sheep dogs also naturally position themselves on the opposite side of the flock from the shepherd and tend to drive them toward him, much as a wolf would head a herd of prey animals toward another member of the pack. Training a dog to herd the sheep away from the shepherd, however, is difficult; that behavior goes against the grain of a natural hunter. Leaving a flock to look for unseen stray individuals is also hard for the dog to learn, for the same reason.

Like wild hunters, sheep dogs improve their performance with experience, becoming invaluable aides to their masters. Losing a good dog can be a disaster to a shepherd, since training a new dog to integrate its instincts with training and experience can be a time-consuming process.

HELPING HUMANS

Today, dogs are trained in centers across America to help

thousands of blind people to lead more normal lives by acting as their eyes, guiding them along busy sidewalks and protecting them from danger. At Guide Dogs for the Blind in San Rafael, California, for example, the dogs receive five months of intensive training before being matched up with a blind person. A variety of problems can interfere with good work. A dog that can't resist chasing a cat, for example, can never be a guide dog. All in all, only about half the dogs that start training go on to become guide dogs.

Once the initial training period is over, the dog is introduced to its blind owner. The dog and owner train together at the center for four challenging weeks, learning how to work together in the real world. They start out by walking on quiet suburban avenues and end up negotiating the busy streets of San Francisco.

A guide dog's most important job is to protect the safety of its owner. It must obey commands given to it to walk forward, turn right or left, and so forth. But since its owner can't see, the person may be unaware of danger, such as a car coming rapidly down the street. The dog must also be aware that it is attached to a taller human at all times. It must avoid an obstacle such as a low-hanging tree branch that won't bother it but that could strike its master. Thus there are times when the dog must disobey its master's orders in order to protect him or her from danger. For this reason—since the dog must make some decisions on its own and sometimes make decisions in direct contradiction to orders it was given—many people feel that guide dogs show special intelligence in their work. Stuart Grout, president of The Seeing Eye in Morristown, New Jersey, says, "I believe that animals think, not like humans think, but in their own terms. And here at The Seeing Eye we have a chance to see that in operation all the time."

Canine Companions in Santa Rosa, California, trains "service dogs," helpmates for handicapped people. These animals act as hands and feet for their owners, pulling their wheelchairs, turning on light switches, and performing other tasks that the handicapped human can't accomplish for himself or herself. Before a young dog at Canine Companions is matched with a handicapped person, it is taught eighty-nine different commands. Then, at "Boot Camp," the dogs are matched up with their new owners, and the two are trained to act as a team. The dogs quickly learn how to work with their individual owners. For example, before boot camp the dogs learn how to fetch items and bring them to a person. Most people are able to reach out and take an item from the dog's mouth. But someone who can barely move the fingers on one hand needs the item brought directly to the hand, so he or she can then grasp it. The service dogs paired with such people learn quickly that just fetching the item isn't enough. They figure out where to place the item so that the person can take it.

HEROIC DOGS

Dogs that guide the blind and service dogs are given a great deal of special training that allows them to perform their remarkable tasks. But what about ordinary dogs? Is dog intelligence merely trainability and eagerness to please, or is there more to it? For example, what about Villa, who rescued her neighbor Andrea from a snowdrift? To hear Andrea tell it, Villa seemed very purposeful in her rescue. She disobeyed by leaping over the five-foot fence surrounding her dog run. After reaching Andrea, she ran around her in circles, which helped clear away the snow. Then she placed her body so that Andrea could grasp her fur while she pulled the girl out and guided her back home through the snow.

Then there's King, a German shepherd mix, that saved his family from a fire in 1981 and was honored by Ken-L Ration for his bravery. King was sleeping in the family room when a fire broke out in the adjoining utility room. Instead of escaping through the open sliding glass doors, King chewed and clawed his way through the wall that separated the family room from the utility room. He dashed through the smoke-filled room and into the bedroom of sixteen-year-old Pearl Carlson. King woke Pearl up by whining and nudging her. The two of them then alerted Mr. and Mrs. Carlson. While Mrs. Carlson and Pearl rushed from the burning house, King helped guide Mr. Carlson, who moved slowly because of a lung condition, to safety.

King had splinters in his mouth from biting through the wall, and he was burned, but his family was safe. In performing his heroic task, King showed not only that he was brave but that he also knew he had to break through that wall and run through the frightening and dangerous fire to get to his family. He understood that the wall separated him from the utility room and the family on the other side.

Ken-L Ration has been giving the Dog Hero award since 1954. Every year many dogs are nominated for the honor, all having rescued people from a variety of perils including traffic accidents, drowning, illness, animal attacks, and burglary, as well as fires and snowstorms. Somehow, these animals recognize dangers to humans and figure out ways to save or protect them. Unfortunately, these sorts of occurrences do not meet the criteria of science. They can't be repeated, and we do not know what mental capabilities allow dogs to behave in these ways. We can just be glad that dogs choose to protect us, whatever the mental basis for this remarkable behavior.

WHAT DOMESTICATION HAS DONE

Wolves live in a world that requires certain predictable kinds of behavior. They must be able to cooperate in the hunt and in caring for their young. Much of their behavior is based on instincts that have served them for countless generations. But wolves must also be able to learn from observation and from their own experience. They may be born with an urge to chase and to bite, but the actual techniques they use to bring down prey cooperatively are learned from watching others in the pack and from practice, much like humans learn a new skill. Experience also helps teach wolves about dangers in their environment, such as steel traps or the guns of hunters.

Over many thousands of years of living with people, dogs have become quite different from their wolf ancestors. Domestication requires the ability to adapt to different surroundings. Some dogs live with human families as pets, with no other dogs around. Others work hard for their human masters, alone or cooperatively in a group. Despite the great variety of circumstances to which dogs are expected to adjust, they usually manage very well to fit into the role expected of them.

THE WOLF AND THE DOG

In order to be able to make these adaptations, dogs have become very flexible; their behavior can easily be molded to fit human needs. A Labrador retriever, for example, can be a family pet, a fine hunting dog, a dog show champion, or a guide dog, with equal success. In the process of adapting to captivity, dogs have also come to depend on humans for their survival and to look to them for food and for meeting their emotional needs. While dogs, like wolves, can form mental maps and can solve problems, a dog generally lacks the independence of the wolf, which enables it to solve certain kinds of problems readily. The dog relies on humans to help it learn what it needs to know, while the wolf counts on itself and on its pack mates for new knowledge. The wolf's mentality serves it well in the wild, and the dog's makes it the ideal helpmate for humans. Both animals have the kind of intelligence they need to survive in the environment in which they live.

Capuchin monkeys, like macaques, can make and use tools. Quincy, an infant capuchin monkey, watches his mother inserting a probe she has made into a hole to obtain sweet syrup. What can we find out about primate learning by studying the way monkeys and apes make and use tools?

—PHOTO BY GREGORY C. WESTERGAARD, FROM *JOURNAL OF COMPARATIVE PSYCHOLOGY* 101:162

6

CLOSEST
TO MAN

Often, those who study animal intelligence are searching for the human reflection in the animal world. They feel that by unraveling the workings of the animal brain, they might find clues to the mysterious minds of humans. And because of their closeness to humankind, they find monkeys and apes especially fascinating.

When people say, "Man descended [or didn't descend] from the monkey," they are misstating evolution. Monkeys and humans are related, but one didn't come from the other. Monkeys, which consist of many different species, share a common ancestor with man and the other apes.

Current theories say that about forty million years ago, the first recognizable ancestors of monkeys and apes appeared. These animals developed a life style different from that of the nocturnal creatures from which they developed. They moved about in the daytime instead of at night, and their eyes became their chief sense as they acquired color vision. Then, around twenty-five million years ago, the ancestors of modern apes separated from the line leading to monkeys and began to evolve in still another direction. While most monkeys stuck to life in the trees, the apes' ancestors spent less time in the forest and more on the savannas, African grasslands with only scattered trees.

Around five million years ago, the ancestors of humans separated from those of other modern apes. The critical difference between these earliest human relations and the other apes was their upright posture. Instead of moving about on all fours much of the time, they stood upright, like modern people.

Humans are very different from apes in many obvious ways, but the relationship is closer than anyone dreamed of before modern genetics came along. When scientists examined the genetic material of humans and apes, they were amazed to find that chimpanzees and humans only differ in 2.5 percent of their DNA. Therefore, humans and chimps are more closely related than chimps and gorillas! The great differences between us and chimpanzees are due to genes that act early in life, regulating how the embryo develops into a fully formed organism.

We've always recognized the similarity of monkeys and apes to ourselves. Expressions such as "You're a monkey's uncle," "I'll make a monkey out of you" and "Monkey see, monkey do" show this awareness. Long before biologists knew just how closely related we were to chimpanzees, these apes were dressed in clothes and taught to imitate human activities such as riding bicycles and smoking cigars. And the research of Jane Goodall into the behavior of wild chimpanzees has shown the strong emotional ties between individuals—ties that recall human attachments.

THE FLEXIBLE MIND

We've already seen that a major component of intelligence lies in flexibility of mind. When things change, when they aren't the way they were before, the intelligent animal notices and tries to adjust to the changed circumstances. The instinctual animal, such as the solitary wasp, sometimes can't adjust, so it continues in its old behavior patterns, even when they don't deal adequately with the new situation. Higher primates—monkeys and apes—are probably the most mentally flexible of all animals. Why should this be the case?

Some investigators think that primate intelligence derives from the nature of its food sources. Primates tend to rely on food that is found in scattered patches, such as fruit that ripens irregularly. They need to be able to remember where they found food yesterday or last week and how to find that place again. This requirement can lead to good learning and memory. For example, when small fruit-eating monkeys called saddleback tamarins were tested in the laboratory, they could remember the locations of thirty separate objects in a room and could recall from day to day which objects were associated with food and which were not. When new objects were introduced, they recognized them right away as novel.

While scattered, complex food sources certainly require good memory, that one factor can't completely explain the primate's adaptability. Other animals, such as some birds, also rely on the same kind of food sources, yet they don't appear to have the mental flexibility of primates.

Other scientists believe that primate intelligence evolved to deal with the complex social life that is characteristic of these gregarious creatures. Over the last thirty years, many researchers have documented the intricate social interactions of primates in the wild. We now know that a monkey or chimpanzee troup is governed by a complicated set of rules and social signals. The need to deal immediately and appropriately with the behavior of one's fellows could certainly result in sharpened wits over time. But other animals, such as zebras and wolves, are also highly social and rely on their group living to help them survive. Even so, such creatures still don't have the great flexibility of mind that characterizes many primate species.

Perhaps the real key, as suggested by Jane Goodall and her associate Hans Kummer, resides rather in what might be considered a weakness of primates when compared to, say, wolves. Wolves are highly efficient killers; they do one thing very well. Monkeys and apes, on the other hand, have no one great skill. They are quite good at a lot of different tasks. While mammals are much more intelligent than insects, there is a parallel here with solitary wasps and honeybees. The wolf is a specialist like the wasp, and the primate is a generalist, like the honeybee. Instinct, which results in less flexible behavior patterns, works like a lock and key. In a particular situation, the behavior is superbly suited to the occasion. But when things change, it is no longer appropriate. The primate brain is designed not to open just one kind of lock especially well; it can figure out how to work many different kinds of locks. Instead of the built-in talents exhibited by many animals, the primate goes about solving life's problems in a flexible, adaptable way.

HOW ONE MONKEY LIVES

Unfortunately, very little is known about the intelligence of primates in the wild. Scientists have studied the behavior of several species in detail, but inferring intelligence from field observations is very difficult. When intelligence shows most, as we've already seen, is often by way of unique occurrences. By nature, such events can't be reproduced, so science balks at using them as evidence. But by looking at one kind of monkey, we can get some idea of where its intellectual strengths and weaknesses lie.

The vervet monkey of East Africa has been studied by many scientists, including Robert M. Seyfarth and Dorothy L. Cheney of the University of Pennsylvania and Thomas T. Struhsaker of Rockefeller University. It lives in groups consisting of several adult males and females, along with their immature young. When they become sexually mature, males leave the group, while females stay and remain close to their own mothers and sisters in social standing. These monkeys spend most of their time in the forest, feeding largely on fruit and insects.

Vervets provide food for several different predators—

leopards, eagles, baboons, pythons, and others—and many lives are lost to such enemies. These monkeys have at least six different alarm calls to warn others in the troop of danger. When one monkey gives out the eagle alarm, the others look up in the air. When the leopard alarm sounds, the animals head for the trees. Thus, each alarm brings a response appropriate to the particular danger of the moment.

Many of these monkeys also respond to the different alarm calls of the starlings that share their habitat. Upon hearing the starling aerial alert, about three-fourths of the monkeys look up, while half run for the trees when the birds give their ground-enemy warning. Since only some of the monkeys pay attention to the starlings' alert, the response is probably learned, not inborn.

Vervets have also learned some other important things about the other creatures with which they live. They seem to know that domesticated cows go along with Masai tribespeople. When the cows appear, the monkeys run away, for the Masai often throw rocks and sticks at the monkeys.

However, the monkeys' ability to associate aspects of their environment with danger is limited. They seem very attuned to sound cues but are not alert to indirect warnings their eyes could see. For example, leopards often stash their prey in trees, so a gazelle carcass hanging over a branch means a leopard might be near. The monkeys, however, pay no attention to this potential clue. The track of a python in the dust also brings on no concern. But if the leopard or python itself shows up, the animals cry an alarm.

Like wolves, vervets are very aware of social status within the band. Each monkey knows its own place and that of every other animal in the group. When researchers played a recording of the screams of a young vervet to a group of females, the mother of that youngster responded most strongly. She knew the voice of her own offspring. But more interesting is the fact that the other females often looked at the mother instead of toward the sound when they heard the recording. They, too, could identify the individual and knew who its mother was.

Vervets know a great deal about social relationships within the troop, but they seem quite dense when it comes to understanding that a python track can mean danger. This sort of discovery makes some biologists think that primate intelligence originated by way of the social life, since that is where they show the greatest sensitivity and adaptability.

NEAREST TO HUMANS

Because of their close relationship to humankind, the great apes—gibbons, orangutans, gorillas, and chimpanzees—are especially important in the study of animal intelligence. By examining these creatures, we can learn what connects us with the rest of the living world as well as what sets us apart.

Until the 1960s, almost nothing was known about the behavior of apes in the wild. To most people, they were amusing creatures to view in the zoo or the circus. No one took them very seriously. But in the late 1950s, the pioneering anthropologist Louis Leakey convinced Jane Goodall, at the time his secretary, to study the behavior of chimpanzees in the wild. Goodall's continuing work at

Tanzania's Gombe Stream Game Preserve has opened our eyes to the intelligence and to the emotional lives of chimpanzees. It has also encouraged scientists to study the natural behavior of other great apes, such as the mountain gorilla and the orangutan. Altogether, this work has increased our knowledge of and our respect for these fascinating animals.

One of Goodall's most important and surprising findings was that chimps make tools. Until her work, anthropologists often set humans apart from other living beings by designating us the "tool-users." While previously a few animals were known to use tools, their behavior seemed instinctive, rather than learned. We've already noted some examples of tool use by birds, and some mammals such as the sea otter use tools as well. This animal will hold a rock on its chest and pound sea urchins and clams on it to break open their shells.

But chimp tool manufacture and use is very complex behavior, and it is learned. The most elaborate tool chimpanzees make is a probe for fishing termites out of their nests. Learning how to make and use a good probe takes plenty of practice. Scientists studying adult chimpanzees have attempted to learn the method but found that the chimps could easily outdo them. Infant chimps start to learn by imitating adults, but it takes years of trial and error before they are good at it.

To make a probe, the chimp breaks off a blade of grass or a twig of the right length and diameter. With a twig, the animal carefully removes any leaves or side branches that might interfere with the probe, using its hands and teeth to shape the tool. Blades of grass are trimmed to the appropriate width before they are inserted into termite nests. Once the tool is ready, the chimp picks at a termite mound with its fingers, making a hole in which it inserts the tool. Inside the nest, defending termites attack the invading probe, biting with their strong jaws and hanging on like bulldogs. The chimp waits for a moment, then pulls the tool and the attached angry termites out, picking them off with its lips. When one tool breaks or bends, the chimp makes a new one until it tires of termite fishing.

Sticks have other uses for chimps. They are stuck into bees' nests, and the honey that clings is licked off. One chimp will use a stick to clean another animal's teeth or to scratch itself. Sticks are poked at potentially dangerous objects such as snakes and are used to rake in food that can't otherwise be reached. Chimps join hollow sticks together to make a stick long enough to reach food. A chimpanzee will even use a small stick to rake in a bigger one if that is what is needed to get at food. In captivity, chimps also show their understanding of how to put objects to work for them. They will stack as many as four boxes in order to reach food. Chimps may even cooperate with one another and work together to move a very heavy box.

Chimps make other tools as well. They bite splinters from the ends of sticks to form a chisel-shaped tool for prying, and they crumple and chew leaves to make sponges for soaking up water from deep inside tree hollows.

Both in the wild and in captivity, chimps show ingenuity in solving problems involving the use of tools. A shy wild chimp that was afraid to take a banana from a person's hand knocked it away with a stick and then picked it up. When one researcher put rocks inside boxes a captive chimp needed, making them too heavy for the animal to move, the chimp removed the rocks, then moved the boxes.

CHIMPS IN GROUPS

Emil W. Menzel of the State University of New York at Stony Brook studied a group of captive chimps in a large outdoor enclosure for five years. Their behavior showed a great deal of creativity and intelligence. One type that ended up causing a great deal of trouble was the use of poles as ladders. At first, the chimps would set a pole upright and climb rapidly to the top, jumping off before it fell. But a few years later, one chimp figured out how to brace a pole against a wall in order to get over it. Using this method, the animals invaded the observation house from which the experimenters watched the animals.

Chimps like to climb in trees, but Menzel had blocked the lower branches of the trees in the enclosure by adding electrified wire so the chimps couldn't get into them. The animals got around the wire by bracing a pole against the wall, climbing it, and pulling it up. Then they braced the pole again and dropped the opposite end into the tree-top. It took the chimps some time to get it just right, but by watching one another and experimenting, all of them eventually learned. Later still, one chimp figured out how to use the pole to escape over the walls of the compound. The other chimps watched, and within a day all eight of them had gotten away.

Menzel performed some experiments with six young chimps that showed their ability to remember the location of objects and to communicate this information to one another. The animals had all been born in the wild but had been living together in the enclosure for a year, so they knew one another well. Menzel's experiments were very simple. He locked five of the chimps in a cage while he carried the sixth into the enclosure, where an object was hidden. Sometimes the item was a snake, which chimps fear. Other times it was food. He showed the animal the hidden object, then carried the chimpanzee back to its companions.

After the investigator had returned to the observation house, the door of the cage was opened by remote control. Then he watched to see what the chimps would do. The animal that knew where the object was almost always led the others right to the hiding place. It had no trouble remembering just where the hidden object lay.

Besides remembering where to head when released, the informed chimp seemed somehow to communicate to its companions what to expect when they arrived at the hiding place. If food had been hidden, the animals seemed eager to get to the site. When the cage door was opened, some of them ran ahead, looking under clumps of grass for food as they went. But if a fake snake had been hidden, the other chimps were more cautious. They tended to take their cues from the leader instead of rushing out on their own. How did the knowledgeable chimp inform his companions whether something desirable—food—or something potentially dangerous—a snake—lay ahead? The researchers believe that the leader didn't make sounds or gestures that got the message across. It seems that its subtle behavior— glances, its manner of walking, its look of apprehension or anticipation—communicated what the other chimps could expect.

Sometimes the food or phony snake was removed. If

food had been there, the knowing animal hunted through the grass with its hands right around the hiding place, searching for the tasty treats. But if a snake had been there, the animal used a stick to probe through the grass. Clearly, the chimp had formed an expectation based on what it had seen hidden earlier in the field.

MONKEYS USE TOOLS

When Jane Goodall discovered that chimpanzees manufacture and use tools, scientists gained new respect for these animals. Since then, however, scientists have also seen monkeys use tools. Macaques, who live in Asia, and cebus monkeys from South America will drop or throw branches and sticks to scare intruders. They also use stones to pound open fruit and nuts. At least one kind of cebus monkey also makes a tool to extract sweet liquid.

Knowing these facts, Gregory C. Westergaard of the University of Washington set out to see if macaques would also make tools given the opportunity. Lion-tailed macaques live in trees and eat a variety of food. They use their hands a great deal and employ objects to create ladders and perches, so he felt they might be able to make and use other sorts of tools as well.

Westergaard devised a cabinet with six holes leading to containers of syrup and placed it in a cage with a group of nine lion-tailed macaques. He noticed that the infants manipulated objects very little, while juvenile monkeys were most curious about them. Adults were not as interested. When the cabinet was first introduced, the syrup level was near the top of each hole, and the monkeys used their fingers to get at it. But as time went on, the level dropped, and fingers were no longer good enough. Most of the animals lost interest at this point. But four of them—one adult female and three juveniles—discovered that they could use a stick to poke at the liquid. Three of the animals figured it out without first trying—they must have thought it through in their minds, much like the wolf pups that got to the food dishes without error. The fourth, which was the youngest of the discoverers, used trial-and-error learning rather than insight.

Like chimpanzees making termite catchers, the macaques detached the sticks and often removed projections that could get in the way. Westergaard found out that the monkeys could also learn by watching one another. He took two youngsters that had figured out how to use sticks to get at the syrup and put them in with another from their group that hadn't done it yet and with two adults who had never been exposed to the setup before. The youngsters had been away from the cabinet for eight months, but they began using sticks to feed right away. On the second day, the two adults followed suit, and on the sixth day the other young monkey joined them.

Tool use isn't the only kind of behavior copied by others. Young vervet monkeys know instinctively how to make the predator warning cries their elders use. But they don't know at first when to use them. A young vervet may give out an eagle warning when an innocent songbird wings overhead. The youngsters seem to learn the warning calls' appropriate use gradually by observing the adults.

Learning by imitation is a powerful method for adapting to the environment. Japanese macaques copy a number of behaviorial patterns from one another or from their human caretakers—rinsing the sand off sweet potatoes in the surf, using water to separate sand from wheat grains, and swimming in the sea.

APE REASONING

The ability to prepare and use tools could be said to require reasoning, and other experiments show that chimps do, indeed, have limited reasoning power. Four chimps were tested in one experiment. They watched while an experimenter hid food in two different places, then while another chimp took the food from one location. When allowed to choose themselves where to get food, the animals almost always chose the location not previously visited. They were able to infer that the food would be gone since another chimp had already been there.

Chimps can also solve more abstract problems. Sarah, a chimp in David Premack's laboratory, learned how to use plastic chips to represent words and concepts. Sarah was given logic problems much like those on some human IQ tests—A is to A′ as B is to what? For example, A might be a medium-sized, blue, saw-toothed shape with marks on it, while A′ was a medium-sized, blue, unmarked saw-toothed-shaped piece. Given B as a large, orange, marked crescent, Sarah would correctly choose a large, orange, unmarked crescent over a large, blue, marked crescent. Sarah was give fifty-two problems of this type, with the differing trait sometimes being color, other times marking, shape, or size. She was correct in her choices 85 percent of the time. Since each problem was unique, Sarah couldn't have learned the right responses. She had to understand how to identify the relationship between the two objects in the first pair and apply that knowledge to solve the problem.

Sarah also knew that one chip meant "same" and another one represented "different." Then she was presented with two sets of items, A and A' and B and B', and asked if the relationship of A to A' was the same as B to B'. On these problems, she scored 72 percent right. She also did well on concept questions (paper is to scissors as apple is to knife or plate? correct answer: knife). This type of question can get quite subtle: lid is to jar as apple is to knife or plate. She got that one right, too, choosing plate. Sarah scored 84 percent correct on these difficult analogy questions.

Her ability to form such comparisons was limited, however. When she was presented with examples of A and A' and then asked to choose an appropriate set, B and B', from a collection of six choices, she couldn't do it. Only once out of eighteen times did Sarah successfully solve this sort of problem. A human being would certainly perform better.

Sarah used her chips for more than solving logic problems. Since each chip represented a word or a concept, the chips could be strung together to form sentences. Sarah could use them to communicate. She was just one chimp trained during the 1970s in some form of symbolic communication.

PART 3
LANGUAGE AND THE MIND

Roger Fouts relaxes with Tatu, one of the
chimps in his group that knows sign language. How well can we communicate with
our close relatives, the great apes, using sign
language? What can we find out about how
they think and feel in this way? What can
such studies tell us about ourselves?

— PHOTO BY FRIENDS OF WASHOE

7

CAN APES UNDERSTAND LANGUAGE?

On June 21, 1966, a revolution in psychology quietly began. On that date, two teachers at the University of Nevada, Beatrix and R. Allen Gardner, began raising a ten-month-old chimpanzee as if it were a human child in a modest trailer behind their home. They named the chimp Washoe. Their goal was to find out how far a chimpanzee could travel across the bridge spanning the gap between human and animal. In the 1950s, other scientists had tried with four different chimps, but they always ran up against a major stumbling block—language. Despite all their attempts to get chimps to communicate with them, the previous investigators had met with silence from their young apes. Only one chimp, named Viki, had managed to utter four words recognizably—"cup," "up," "mama," and "papa"—despite seven years of being surrounded by the English language and after intensive teaching efforts. These results were used again and again as proof that an unbridgeable gap separated humans from other animals. We could use language, and they could not. As long as that seemed to be true, people could continue to feel comfortably superior to the other creatures with which they shared the earth.

The Gardners, however, had a different attitude. They still believed there must be a way to reach across the gap and communicate with chimpanzees, our closest animal cousins. They chose not to be discouraged by the failure of others. One day, while watching tapes of one of these animals in action, they realized that they could lip-read what the chimp was saying, although the sounds that came out didn't resemble human speech. Maybe the problem didn't lie in the chimps' ability to learn and use language. With the sound on the tape turned off, it was clear that the chimp could imitate the lip movements of human speakers. Maybe the difficulty was that the vocal apparatus of chimps couldn't handle human speech. After all, wild chimps are usually silent unless they are excited. They are far more likely to wave their arms about than to make sounds.

FINDING A WAY TO TALK
The Gardeners decided to try something different with Washoe. Instead of speaking to her, they communicated by using a modified version of American Sign Language

(ASL), the gestural language used by the deaf in North America. ASL, also called Ameslan, communicates words and ideas through arm and hand movements. One or both hands may be used. Some "words" consist simply of pointing, as for parts of the body. But most have a standard form. The word for fruit, for example, is expressed by putting one fist along the side of the mouth. Word order doesn't have the importance in ASL that it has in English; much of the meaning is conveyed through facial expressions and by small variations in the ways the signs are made.

Washoe's trailer was a quiet place, the silence broken only by the sounds of clattering toys and dishes and of footsteps both human and chimpanzee. The Gardners used ASL in the same way a human parent would speak to a baby—to point out pictures in a book and to identify the sights and sounds of Washoe's home and neighborhood. Visitors were forbidden to speak aloud, which proved a real hardship to many. But it was important for Washoe to experience gestures as the accepted means of communication.

Washoe thrived in this very unapelike environment. She learned how to get herself dressed and undressed, how to brush her teeth, how to sit at the table and eat with a fork and spoon. Washoe drank from a cup and used the toilet. She enjoyed looking through picture books and magazines and fondled her doll the way a human child would. And all along, she learned to "talk" in much the same way a human child does—by imitating the adults who shared her world. Like a human child, she was encouraged and aided in learning to form "words" in the right way. By the time Washoe knew eight signs, she began combining them in apparently meaningful ways—when a dog barked, she signed "listen dog." Her doll was "baby mine," and her potty chair, "dirty good."

After fifty-one months, Washoe reliably used at least 132 signs. Like a human child, she easily extended the meaning of a sign beyond specific examples. She knew a dog was a dog, whatever its size or color, and the same was true for the other objects in her environment. She also made some interesting errors. After learning the sign for "flower," for example, Washoe generalized it to odors, such as cigar smoke, rather than to other flowers. The Gardners seemed to have hit the jackpot with Washoe, opening up the possibilities for all sorts of exciting research. But unfortunately, human nature intervened to confuse matters and to undermine the importance of what Washoe and the Gardners had accomplished.

The Gardners' success initially created a great deal of excitement. While newspapers and popular magazines heralded the arrival of the talking ape and speculated wildly about future possibilities, scientists were more cautious. They had a hard time deciding how to view the Gardners' work. Science is generally carried out through carefully planned experiments that can be reliably repeated or by detailed, detached observation of the natural world. But the Gardners had used neither of these methods. They jumped right in and treated Washoe as if she were human. They purposely avoided rigid experiments—after all, what parents experiment on their developing children? And their observations of Washoe could hardly be considered uninvolved. While the chimp did sign to herself, to her doll, and to other animals, the significance of her communication lay mainly in her communication with her human "parents." They participated intimately with their subject instead of being unobtrusive observers.

The Gardners used sign language because they wanted to make the chimp's environment as close as possible to that of a human child. They were interested in the total intellectual capacity of chimps and in finding a way to compare it with that of humans. Since language skills are such a vital part of our intellectual makeup, the chimps had to have a way of communicating back and forth with humans in a natural human language. ASL met this need.

The Gardners' work with Washoe didn't meet the strict criteria of scientific experimentation or observation because such was not their goal. They were not focusing on the chimp's ability to use language. But the lack of objectivity, even though intentional, allowed critics to have a field day, tearing apart their work and finding flaws at every turn. The importance of the breakthrough in interspecies communication got lost in the barrage of criticism. Despite the criticisms, the Gardners expanded their work, adding other chimps and new scientists to their project. Roger Fouts, who received his Ph.D. for work on Project Washoe, took Washoe with him in 1971 when he moved to the Institute for Primate Studies in Oklahoma. There, ape and scientist continued to work together.

In the wake of Washoe, other scientists as well tried their hands at teaching chimps language. Some worked with ASL. Others tried different techniques that involved less interaction between trainer and ape and that were felt to be more easily quantified. These researchers feared that too much about the ASL work was subjective. There was room for error in interpreting which sign a chimp was making. And since the chimps were signing to people and people were interpreting the signs, they felt that unconscious cues could be passing from human to ape and from ape to human, making the learning of the animals hard to evaluate.

But some critics, having warmed up on Washoe and the Gardners, managed to find fault in every ape language study. While many criticisms of ape language research are valid, some seem almost hysterical. Perhaps it is difficult for some people to let go of the notion that language is the one thing that makes humans unique in the living world; they are reluctant to give up that feeling and will fight against whatever threatens it.

WHAT IS LANGUAGE?
All sorts of animals communicate with one another. Some organisms, such as ants, use scent to convey the presence of danger or the location of food. Others, like birds, use their voices to announce their territory. But such "languages" only contain a few relatively simple messages. They have nothing like the vocabulary of a human tongue. We've seen the complex "language" of bees in action, showing the way to a valuable food source. Bee communication may be amazing and elegant, but it doesn't use a true language in the human sense. A bee is born knowing how to "talk" and knowing the meanings of the "words"; the language is inherited.

Human languages are so different from those of other animals that no one worried about how to define a true language before the experiments with chimpanzees. Only humans had language, so it needed no precise definition.

But, as one group of researchers put it, "With Washoe's first words, the definition of language suddenly became an issue of the first order."

One thing that sets human languages apart is that they are completely learned. Only the ability to speak using complex, subtle sounds and the ability to acquire language are inherited. From then on, it's up to culture. Your native tongue is determined by what those around you speak as you grow up.

Human languages have evolved and changed through use over the centuries until today there are over 400 different ones. Even though they vary a great deal, they share certain traits. They all have individual words that stand for objects and actions. Other words function as further descriptions of these objects and actions. Each language also has an internal structure, its own way of arranging the words so that a listener can understand the meanings of the words in a particular sentence. In English, for example, the first noun in a sentence is generally the subject, followed by the verb, with the object of that verb at the end. It is easy to distinguish between the two sentences, "The man chased the dog," and "The dog chased the man." The order of the words determines the meaning. This "grammar" of a language is called its syntax. We may think of English word order as the logical one, but other languages use endings added onto words to indicate whether they are subjects or objects. The endings, rather than the word order, indicate the role of the word in the sentence. In German, for example, whether "man" or "dog" came first wouldn't matter; the listener could tell which was the subject and which the object on the basis of word endings.

USING LANGUAGE

We have no doubt that humans communicate by means of languages. We also know that some animals can learn to understand words, and a few can even speak to their human trainers. But are such animals really using language in the sense that we use it? This is a very difficult question to answer. The key to true language in this sense is knowing the intention of the "speaker." Is the speaker really trying to tell us something? When a dog scratches at the door, is it trying to communicate that it wants to go out? Or is it merely aware that when it scratches, someone will open the door? When a ape signs "Give orange," is it trying to convey a desire, or does it merely know that using those signs will result in getting an orange?

The term "linguistic" is used to distinguish true language from other forms of communication, such as that of the bees or of a human using pantomime to communicate. Linguistic communication utilizes learned words and syntax. Symbols—words—are used consciously to represent actions, objects, and descriptions. The difficult thing is finding out whether an animal is using symbols consciously or just performing behavior that will get rewards.

DO APES COMMUNICATE LINGUISTICALLY?

No one can argue that apes can be taught to communicate with humans and even with one another using ASL. But many pages have been filled with the debate over how much the apes actually understand. Are they just learning the meaning of individual words, the way a trained animal might, and then spouting them back to their trainers? Or can apes really understand the concept of syntax and use it in the same way human children do? No one imagines that the apes could ever learn to use language like adult humans do, to compose poetry or describe the structure of the atom. But whether they are in a separate class from humans, unable to understand the concept of language, or whether they are intelligent enough to grasp the rudiments of linguistic communication is at the root of the controversy. Unfortunately, this question can't be satisfactorily answered yet, for people have not yet found agreement on how to define the word "language." But just considering the controversy and the different opinions about chimps and language can teach us some important things about the nature of language, intelligence, and human nature.

By the time a chimp raised in a humanlike environment is about a year old, its language ability is about the same as that of a year-old child. The chimp, like many human one-year-olds, makes one- and two-word statements about its immediate environment—"Gimme drink," or "There diaper," for example. And like a child, the chimp will voluntarily use language to begin an interaction with a human by asking questions and making requests. These chimps even talk to themselves as does a human baby left to its own devices. The Gardners describe Washoe:

[She] . . . often signed to herself in play, particularly in places that afforded her privacy, i.e., when she was high in the tree or alone in her bedroom before going to sleep . . . Washoe also signed to herself when leafing through magazines and picture books, and she resented our attempts to join in this activity. If we did try to join her or if we watched her too closely, she often abandoned the magazine . . . Washoe not only named pictures to herself in this situation, but she also corrected herself.

Washoe also signed to herself about her own on-going or impending actions. We have often seen Washoe moving stealthily to a forbidden part of the yard, signing *quiet* to herself.

Also like human children, chimps learning ASL invent their own words to describe new experiences. Lucy, an-other chimp who learned ASL, invented a new sign to refer to the leash used when she went on walks. Washoe de-veloped her own sign for the bib that she wore. The chimps raised by the Gardners would also combine signs to create new words—"metal hot" for a cigarette lighter; "metal cup drink coffee" meant a Thermos bottle; "listen drink" re-ferred to the fizzing of Alka Seltzer. The chimp Lucy used modifiers to categorize objects in the same class such as fruits: oranges and lemons were "smell fruits," while a watermelon was called a "candy fruit" or a "drink fruit." After tasting a hot radish, Lucy dubbed it a "hurt fruit" or a "cry fruit."

Despite the various examples of chimps inventing words for new objects, some scientists just don't believe chimps can understand language deeply enough to use it in this fashion. An example of this type of criticism is the con-troversy over Washoe's dubbing a swan a "water bird." Critics, such as Herbert Terrace of Columbia University, claim that Washoe was merely answering the question "What that?" posed by her trainers. They claim she was re-ferring to two things she saw at the same time, water and a bird. However, the description of how Washoe used the term indicates something quite different. As her companion, scientist Roger Fouts, described the situation, "I often take Washoe for boat rides in a pond surrounding a chimpanzee island at the Institute. The pond is inhabited by two very territorial and nasty swans. Since I do not have a sign for swan, I refer to them with the *duck* sign. Washoe does not have the *duck* sign in her vocabulary, so she refers to the swans as *water birds*." Even when the swans are out of the water, Washoe would call them "water birds," so that clearly was her name for them, a name she herself had invented.

Fouts relates another incident involving Washoe, one in which she expanded the meaning of a word she already knew in much the same way a human child might do:

> I was about to teach Washoe the sign *monkey* and while I was preparing the data sheet she turned around and began to interact with a particularly obnoxious macaque in a holding cage behind us. They threatened each other in the typical chimpanzee and macaque manner. After I had prepared the data sheet I stopped the aggressive interaction and turned her around so that she was facing two siamangs [small apes that look like monkeys]. I asked her what they were in ASL. She did not respond. After I molded her hands into the correct position for the *monkey* sign three times she began to refer to the siamangs with the *monkey* sign. I interspersed questions referring to various objects that she had signs for in her vocabulary. Next, I turned her toward the adjacent cage holding some squirrel monkeys and she transferred the *monkey* sign immediately to them. After she called the squirrel monkeys *monkey* several times I turned her around and asked her what her previous adversary was, the macaque, and she con-

sistently referred to him as a *dirty monkey*. Up until this time she had used the *dirty* sign to refer to feces and soiled items; in other words as a noun. She had changed the usage from a noun to an adjective. In essence, it could be said that she had generated an insult. Since that time she has similarly used the dirty sign to refer to me as *dirty Roger* once when I signed to her that I couldn't grant her request to be taken off the chimpanzee island *(out me)* and another time she asked for some fruit *(fruit me)* and I signed *sorry but I not have any fruit.* Lucy has also used the *dirty* sign in a similar manner. Once she referred to a strange cat she had been interacting with aggressively as a *dirty cat,* and she has also referred to a leash (which she dislikes) as a *dirty leash.*

What Washoe did here is impressive. She created her own insult and used it in a variety of situations to express her displeasure. Such a creative use of language implies understanding beyond rote learning.

Another objection of ape language critics is that the apes do not use a consistent word order when they string signs together. Some of the apes in some situations understand the meanings of individual signs and use them liberally. But in order to show an understanding of syntax, the apes should put the words in the correct order. Terrace analyzed chimp utterances to see if word order was consistent, and it was not. Terrace claims this lack of syntax shows that the chimps do not demonstrate "linguistic competence." But other scientists object to his conclusion, pointing out that this lack does not mean that the apes are not really using language when they use signs. For one thing, word order doesn't have the importance in ASL that it has in

English, especially in short sentences such as those used by chimps. And in this inattention to word order, as in their other behavior, they are like human children in the early stages of learning. Anyone who has been around human children as they begin to learn language knows that they don't use consistent word order at first, even though they are clearly consciously using words appropriately. Scientific studies bear out this conclusion. Chimps might not be capable of getting past this stage of communication, but that doesn't mean they have no concept of the symbolic meaning of words.

Even though they lack the correct use of syntax, chimps can show through their use of ASL a surprising understanding of the world around them. Scientists have tried to discover ways of finding out what goes on in animal minds; getting animals to talk back to us in words we understand can give us a window on their world. Do animals remember about how to utilize things that are out of their sight? How long can they remember? Some clues to these questions, at least for one chimpanzee, can be gained from the following conversation between Washoe and one of her human friends:

George: What you want?
Washoe: Orange, orange.
George: No more orange, what you want?
Washoe: Orange.
George: (Getting angry) No more orange, what you want?
Washoe: You go car gimme orange. Hurry.

Although Washoe had not ridden in a car for over two years, she seemed to remember that people go in cars to stores where they can buy food and bring it back to give to hungry chimps. Clearly, Washoe had a great deal of understanding of how the human world operates, and she could remember things for a long time.

KOKO, THE TALKING GORILLA

In 1972, a Stanford University graduate student named Penny Patterson began to teach ASL to a year-old gorilla named Koko. The two have been together ever since. Now Koko is at the center of the continuing controversy over ape language experiments. Instead of performing her work in a university setting, Dr. Patterson has her own private institute funded largely by private citizens through the Gorilla Foundation. For an annual membership fee, subscribers receive a journal that details "conversations" with Koko and with Michael, a younger male gorilla that is also learning ASL. While scientists generally publish carefully designed experiments in scientific journals, Dr. Patterson presents her data largely through her journal, "Gorilla," and in the popular press. Edited versions of interactions with the gorillas are all that the public normally sees. The lack of controlled experiments and the way in which the information is presented make it impossible to evaluate Koko's achievements.

Patterson claims many accomplishments for Koko. According to her, Koko knows over 500 signs and makes statements averaging three to six signs long. She says that Koko not only talks about objects in her environment but also describes her feelings. In early 1988, for example, Dr. Patterson announced that Koko had expressed a desire to give birth to a gorilla baby. Michael, according to Dr. Patterson, has described how poachers killed his mother in Africa when he was two years old. Without any real scientific experiments behind them, such claims only serve to increase the negative attitude of skeptical scientists toward the language abilities of apes.

Unfortunately, Koko doesn't respond well to all the lights, sounds, and general confusion that surround taping or filming. Thus, her accomplishments do not come across well when taped or filmed. As the author Eugene Linden describes Koko in his book about ape language, *Silent Partners:*

> Visitors see a gorilla who uses her several-hundred-word vocabulary to tell stories, escape blame, make jokes, tell fibs, understand her surroundings, and relate to her human and gorilla companions. . . . Most of her jokes seem to be attempts to sabotage what Koko considers to be boring drills and conversations. For instance, if Koko is bored or feeling obstreperous, she will vary the way a sign is made and, in so doing, subtly change its meaning. Once when asked too many times to make the "drink" sign (which is made by placing to the lips a thumb extended from a closed fist), Koko responded by making the sign in her ear. Another time, when shown bottles, she made the appropriate sign on her nose and then signed, "Funny there."

It is too bad that Koko and Michael's accomplishments can't be evaluated scientifically. But the ape language controversy became so intense during the late 1970s that grants for research dried up. Going private was the only way Patterson could continue her work, and the negativism of the critics discouraged her from trying to publish her research in scientific journals any longer. Her decision is unfortunate for the study of animal language capabilities.

LEGACY OF CONTROVERSY

Patterson's work with Koko wasn't the only victim of the controversy over ape language experiments. Other projects collapsed as well. The critics of the work not only pointed out problems with the design of the experiments, but they also blasted the whole endeavor. Instead of suggesting ways to improve the experiments, they often ridiculed everything about the work. The apes and scientists alike were left with no place to go. Some scientists got out of this kind of research altogether, fearing that their reputations would be damaged if they continued. As a consequence, many exciting projects were never completed.

Roger Fouts had planned to place a group of signing chimps in a large enclosure and encourage them to set up a cooperative society with its own economic system. Such an experiment would have tested very interesting aspects of the similarity between chimps and humans. At the time ape language research collapsed, a few young chimps were learning sign language from older chimps rather than from people. It would have been very interesting to see how far chimps could go in teaching one another ASL and in communicating by way of signs. All of the chimps to be utilized in the experiments had been using ASL for just a few years and were only working with it a few hours a day. Human children, however, are immersed in language all their waking hours from the time they are born. How far might chimps have gone with human language if they had been exposed more intensively?

CAN APES UNDERSTAND LANGUAGE?

Fortunately, a few scientists besides Penny Patterson still continue to study the language abilities of apes, despite the hazards to their scientific reputations. They strive to avoid the problems of the earlier language work. Sue Savage-Rumbaugh at the Yerkes Primate Center studies how two chimps, named Sherman and Austin, converse with each other by way of computer. The two animals are in separate rooms, and every communication is recorded. That way, their "conversations" cannot be influenced by body language or other nonlanguage cues, and everything they "say" to one another can easily be analyzed.

One of the most serious problems with determining how much the apes understand about what they are doing is that most of the evidence of what they do is derived from anecdotes, such as Lucy's invention of new signs and Washoe's request that her human companion go in the car to fetch oranges. This type of behavior is not reliably repeatable; it can't be verified by experiments.

Savage-Rumbaugh and her coworkers found a way to test whether chimps can remember objects that aren't present in the room and whether they can communicate their intentions using word symbols to a person. The setup is as follows: The chimpanzee is in a room with a keyboard. The keys on the keyboard have symbols representing objects instead of letters and numbers. Outside the room is a tray with various objects on it. The chimpanzee goes to the tray and looks at the items. Then it uses the keyboard to select the symbol for one of the items on the tray. It then goes back to the tray, picks up the item, and hands it to a human observer. The observer then checks to see whether the item the chimp gave him was the same as the one whose symbol was selected on the keyboard. In order to perform correctly on this task, the chimp must first remember at least one item that was on the tray so it can choose an appropriate symbol. Then it must remember which item it chose when it goes back to the tray, select that item, and, finally, give it to the observer. The task may not seem like a difficult one, but it shows that a chimp can have an intention. By indicating an object on the keyboard and then taking it to the observer, the chimp is communicating, "This is the item I am going to select from the tray." It is also showing that it can connect the item with the symbol when both aren't present at the same time.

When ape language research funds dried up, the Institute for Primate Studies could no longer keep its chimps. Roger Fouts and his wife, Debbi, moved with Washoe to Central Washington University in Ellensburg, Washington. Washoe now lives in a group of five chimps. One of them, a young male named Loulis, has learned seventy-seven signs from his adoptive mother Washoe and the other chimps in the group, all of whom had learned ASL from the Gardners. The chimps use ASL to communicate with one another as well as with their human caretakers.

H. Lyn Miles at the University of Tennessee has taught an orangutan named Chantek over a hundred signs. Chantek has also learned to work for tokens to "spend" later on treats. She appears to understand that by cleaning up her room, she will be "paid" so that she can buy things she wants. Thus, an orangutan seems to have learned the concept of work in the present for reward in the future.

AN APE "GENIUS"?
Sue Savage-Rumbaugh and her colleagues are also working with a pygmy chimpanzee named Kanzi, a member of a

rare species said to be more like humans than any other ape species. From the time Kanzi was six months old until his mother was sent back to a breeding colony when he was two and a half, Kanzi was with his mother as she was trained in sign language and the keyboard language of symbols. While he picked up some gestures and tried to imitate human speech, he showed almost no interest in the keyboard work his mother was doing.

When Kanzi's mother left, the researchers began to teach him to use the keyboard. To their surprise, the little ape had learned a great deal about the keyboard symbols just by watching his mother at work. Within a week, it became clear that he knew the meaning of many symbols. Not only that, but he used them not just to indicate what he wanted at the moment; he also "talked" about absent objects. The common chimpanzees such as Sherman and Austin that were taught by the group had needed special training to understand these more complex aspects of language, but Kanzi seemed to understand them merely by observation.

Because Kanzi was so adept with language and so eager to use it, the entire program for his training was changed. No active molding or training was used to "teach" symbols to Kanzi. Normally, animals receive rewards such as food when they are successful. This practice reinforces their desire to perform correctly the next time around. But Kanzi learned without overt rewards. He learned spontaneously, more like a human child than a trained ape. Within six months, Kanzi understood the meaning of almost thirty symbols on the keyboard. He was also acquiring an understanding of spoken English, something that Sherman and Austin had never picked up, even though spoken language was used around them all along (see table).

Correct Responses (in percent)

	Keyboard Symbol	Spoken English
Kanzi	95	89
Sherman	99	50
Austin	98	59

A totally chance score would be 43 percent.

At this point, no one can say just how much apes really understand of language. Some researchers are convinced that the animals can comprehend syntax, while others believe they have no concept of how to string "words" into real sentences. What may be needed is a completely new approach to teaching language to apes. The most serious problem to be overcome is how to get the apes to cooperate without the researchers becoming too subjectively involved in the experiments. It is difficult enough for scientists to try to be as objective as possible in research that doesn't deal with such intimate interaction with their material. But chimpanzees and gorillas are very social animals, and there is no point in communicating in the absence of a social meaning; communication is, after all, a means of expressing needs, wants, and other information to another being.

None of the apes in these experiments, however, showed much creativity in their use of language. Some of them invented new signs, but that's about it. The animals always stuck to concrete reality in their utterances. They were interested in food, play, and new things that they encountered in their world. Even a young child, however, can go beyond the material world with his or her limited language skills—for example, by inventing stories and by enjoying the fantasies written by others.

FATE OF THE APES

When funds for ape language research were cut off, it was unfortunate for science. But it was a genuine disaster for most of the animals involved. Chimps are expensive animals to maintain in captivity, and the laboratories could no longer afford to keep them when the money dried up. The chimps had learned how to communicate with humans. Sign language had become an integral part of their lives, and they had become accustomed to being exposed to interesting surroundings and to having close social interactions with people. But this life, relatively rich for a captive animal, couldn't continue without financial support. Most of the language-trained chimps were sold to medical research laboratories, where they had to live in individual cages and be deprived of the opportunity to use their ability to communicate with another species. Only a few, like Washoe and Loulis, were lucky enough to be able to continue their language development and to maintain close ties with the humans they had come to know and depend upon.

The bottle-nosed dolphin, Ake, is responding—correctly—to hand signals from her
trainer to follow an instruction she has
never heard before. Can dolphins be taught
to understand language and its grammar? If
so, what does this tell us about the nature
of language and communication?

—PHOTO BY LOUIS HERMAN, KEWALO
BASIN MARINE MAMMAL LABORATORY

8

LANGUAGE
IN THE SEA

Many criticisms of ape language studies concentrate on the question of whether language production—"saying" things—is necessarily linked to language comprehension—understanding things. The chimp signing "banana" may not understand that the sign it makes represents the object, a banana. It may just realize that if it moves its arms in a certain way, it will get a banana. Since the apes don't do a good job of incorporating syntax into their language use, some scientists have claimed that the animals don't understand the concept of syntax. This conclusion isn't necessarily valid. A human child understands the difference between the sen-

137

tences, "Give the cookie to Mommy," and "Mommy will give the cookie to you," before he or she can speak either sentence. But still, the problem of whether many of the apes that learned signs really understood the symbolic nature of language is a real one.

Louis Herman of the University of Hawaii studied the ape language work carefully and came up with a completely different way of approaching the question of animals' ability to understand language. He decided to work with dolphins and to begin with language understanding by itself, without combining it with how well dolphins might produce language. Recording an animal's response to language commands eliminates many of the pitfalls of interpreting signs made by the animals themselves and is a more objective way to evaluate language learning. It can provide a good starting point in evaluating the language capabilities of a species. Once their ability to understand has been studied, the critical experiments on language production can follow.

Dolphins are completely marine mammals closely related to whales. Unlike seals and walruses, dolphins never leave the water. They are born, grow up, and die beneath the waves. Over the eons, these graceful creatures have evolved to fit exquisitely into their special place in nature. Unlike most mammals, dolphins lack hair, which would slow them down as they swam. They keep their bodies warm instead with an insulating fat layer called blubber. Because of the differences between water and air, dolphins do not interact with their environment in the same way we do. Although we communicate with one another chiefly through sound, sight is our most important sense. We gain most of our information about the world around us through our eyes. In the water, however, light doesn't penetrate very deeply, but sound can carry for miles. Instead of using their eyes to find their way about, dolphins rely on their ears. They have a highly evolved sonar system that allows them to "see" their environment with their ears. As it swims, a dolphin emits a rapid series of high-pitched clicking sounds. When the clicks encounter an object, they bounce back like an echo from the wall of a canyon. The details of how they bounce back depend on the shape and composition of the object. When the echo returns to the dolphin, the animal can interpret very accurately the nature, size, and distance of the object in the environment.

In addition to the sonar clicks, dolphins make other clicking sounds, as well as whistles. These sounds are believed to be used by the dolphins to communicate with one another. Certain sounds are known to contain information. For example, each bottle-nosed dolphin has a unique "signature whistle," which is different from that of other dolphins. Individual animals can identify the signature whistles of dolphins they know.

Unfortunately, we know almost nothing about dolphin communication. When dolphins are chattering, they don't generally open their mouths. The sounds are made within complex air passages in the animals' heads instead of with a voice box and tongue. Thus, a scientist listening to a dolphin "conversation" as the animals swim about in an oceanarium can have difficulty telling which animal is making which sounds. The fact that some of the sounds are too high-pitched for us to hear only complicates matters.

People have known for a long time, however, that dolphins are especially intelligent animals. We may not know how complex their communication systems are, but we do know that dolphins are eager, curious, and enthusiastic students and catch on to new tricks very quickly. Because of their intelligence and trainability and because scientists suspect that they have a relatively sophisticated way of communicating with one another, dolphins seem an ideal subject for language learning experiments.

CREATING ARTIFICIAL LANGUAGES

Herman wanted to deal with several different issues in his dolphin research. The first question was how to avoid the problems encountered in the ape language studies. All of those experiments focused on the ability of animals to produce language. How much they were able to understand of what was "said" to them was not specifically investigated. If the ape gave an appropriate response to a question posed by the researcher, it was assumed that the animal understood the question. No one tested the apes to find out whether they understood the syntax of sentences, or whether the degree of sentence complexity affected their comprehension.

In the 1950s and 1960s, John Lilly tried to teach dolphins how to speak English. His unsuccessful attempts brought plenty of criticism from other scientists aware of the pitfalls of trying to get dolphins to produce language. Herman, therefore, decided to study the dolphins' understanding of artificial languages "spoken" to them.

How could he demonstrate that the animals actually

understood what was being said? Herman began by teaching the animals individual "words" for objects in their tank and for actions, such as fetch or touch. Then the objects were paired with a command for action—fetch the ball or touch the Frisbee.

In order to learn as much as possible from the studies, Herman invented two different languages that were taught to two different dolphins. A dolphin named Phoenix learned a language consisting of whistle-like tones generated by machine and emitted through an underwater speaker. Each tone represented a different word. Akeakamai (Ake for short) was taught a gestural language in which movements of a trainer's hands and arms represented words. In order to see the trainer, Ake had to poke her head out of the water. By using languages requiring different senses—sight and hearing—Herman was able to test the general language ability of the dolphins.

The two languages differed in another very important way. Since there had been so much argument over an animal's ability to comprehend syntax, Dr. Herman used different syntax for the two languages. Phoenix's acoustic language had a grammar similar to English: a sentence was constructed of direct object + action + indirect object. Ake's gestural language, however, was put together differently. For her, the order was indirect object + direct object + action. For example, the "word" order "ball take hoop" meant "Take the ball to the hoop" for Phoenix. For Ake, however, the same meaning would be conveyed by "hoop ball take."

The scientists were careful in their experimental setup to avoid giving the animals cues about what was expected of them. The trainer giving Ake her commands wore goggles to keep from providing any hints of where in the tank the dolphin should swim. The tank-side trainer working with Phoenix did not know what tones the dolphin heard underwater. After the animal responded, an observer who didn't know what command had been given called out what action the dolphin took. If the observer's sentence was the same as the one the animal had been given, the dolphin's action was recorded as correct.

During early training, each animal learned a tone that corresponded to her name and another tone that meant "Yes—you carried out the task correctly." They were also taught a number of action and object words that could be combined into two-word commands. When a dolphin succeeded in performing correctly, the underwater speaker gave out the tones for "yes Phoenix (or Ake) fish," and the trainer gave the dolphin a fish to eat.

Once the dolphins had mastered two-word sentences, the syntax of their languages was made more complex. New words, such as "in," "over," and "under," were added that allowed for more complicated sentences. In addition, Ake was taught the difference between "right" and "left," while Phoenix learned "bottom" and "surface." Understanding these words allowed the sentences to refer to particular items, such as the Frisbee on Ake's left, when more than one Frisbee was in the tank. The animals also learned to relate one object to another. Instead of being told "Frisbee fetch," Phoenix could be asked, for example, "left Frisbee fetch ball"—take the Frisbee on your left to the ball. That sentence could be reversed as well—"ball fetch left Frisbee"—take the ball to the Frisbee on your left. If Phoenix could respond correctly to both commands, it would show she understood that changing the order of the words in a command altered its meaning.

After a great deal of intensive training, each dolphin demonstrated that she could respond correctly to the language she had learned. Phoenix got 91.7 percent of the responses correct on sentences consisting of a modifier + direct object + action (e.g., "surface hoop tail-touch"). Her scores for other types of sentences were all over 65 percent correct, except for five-word sentences such as "bottom pipe fetch surface Frisbee"—take the pipe on the bottom to the Frisbee on the surface. She got 57 percent correct with five-word sentences. Ake made more errors—her scores ranged from 50 percent to 77 percent correct. But all the animals' scores were far above chance. Random guessing at what was wanted with the five-word sentences would lead to only about 4 percent correct responses.

Neither dolphin had much trouble with choosing the correct direct object in sentences that could be reversed. Phoenix picked up the proper object to carry more than 94 percent of the time, while Ake succeeded over 95 percent of the time. Both animals seemed to have more difficulty with indirect objects and their modifiers than with other elements of the sentences. For Ake, indirect objects were especially troublesome—after all, she had to keep the indirect object in her memory while she searched for and obtained the direct object. Phoenix, on the other hand, could take off from her station and head for the direct object before hearing the rest of the sentence. As she was on her way to fetch something, she could find out where to take it.

Ake's language understanding was remarkable for another reason. When she was watching the presentation of a sentence by her trainer, she didn't know at the time the first object symbol was presented what role it would take in the sentence. If the next word was an action, then the first object was a direct object—"ball toss," for example. However, if the next word was another object or a modifier of an object, the first word functioned as an indirect object, as in "ball left Frisbee fetch"—take the Frisbee to the ball on your left. Ake showed little difficulty figuring out the role of objects in the sentences, indicating that she understood the meaning of word order in the sentences.

These responses were all to novel sentences—ones the dolphins had never heard before. They hadn't been trained to carry out specific tasks in the usual fashion of performing animals. Instead, they learned individual words and were able to understand new sentences that combined the familiar words in unique ways. They showed that they comprehended both the meanings of the individual words and the significance of their order in the sentences. As a matter of fact, in the reversible sentences, Phoenix made only one error of reversing the two objects in eighty-five trials, while Ake made no errors for the forty-eight such sentences given to her. Everything was accomplished in challenging surroundings—an outdoor tank with many objects floating in it. The dolphins had to find and choose the correct item as the items were moved about by the wind and the currents made by the swimming dolphins. While carrying out the task, the dolphins themselves also changed positions. This switching made Ake's job especially difficult when following a command such as "left ball hoop fetch." She had to note which ball was to her left when the command was given, swim over to the hoop, and take the hoop to that particular ball, even if it might no longer be on her left.

HINTS ABOUT HOW DOLPHINS THINK

Like apes, dolphins show spontaneous problem-solving that isn't repeatable. Unfortunately, there is no acceptable way to integrate such unique examples into the structure of scientific knowledge. But they can tell us a great deal about how animals solve problems and how they see their world.

Phoenix's responses to commands involving "bottom hoop" clearly show her problem-solving ability. When told "bottom hoop thru," Phoenix dove, only to find the hoop lying flat on the bottom. This was no obstacle to the dolphin. She poked her beak under the edge of the hoop until one side was lifted off the bottom. Then she swam through it.

"Bottom hoop under" was a bit more difficult for Phoenix. Her way of swimming under an object was to turn upside down before swimming beneath it. After diving, she turned upside down, lifted up one edge of the hoop, and swam through it upside down. For this response she got no fish reward. The next time she was told "bottom hoop under," she swam down and raised both sides of the hoop before successfully swimming under rather than through it.

Phoenix also successfully solved other problems involving bottom objects. When asked "bottom pipe toss," she dove down, picked up the pipe, brought it to the surface, then tossed it in the air. For "bottom pipe spit," she positioned herself directly over the pipe and spit into the air.

Once, the dolphins showed more ingenuity than the experimenters. At a point in the tests, the scientists wanted to see how the animals responded to impossible requests. One sentence they felt was impossible to carry out was "water toss" ("water" referred to the flow into the tank from a suspended hose). "Toss" had always been used for objects the dolphins could pick up, so "water toss" seemed an impossible command. However, when Ake was given that sentence, she swam over to the hose and jerked her head through the flow, thus "tossing" the water! The observer, who didn't know what command was given, had no trouble labeling the behavior "water toss." When Phoenix was later asked to "water toss," she responded in the same way as Ake. From then on, "water toss" was added to the dolphins' repertoire.

The dolphins also showed understanding of their languages when given unusual sentences. Phoenix was told "Frisbee fetch thru hoop" once and "Frisbee fetch under hoop" another time. In each case she behaved appropriately, picking up the Frisbee and swimming through or under the hoop. When given the instruction "Frisbee fetch thru gate," she carried the Frisbee through the gate, instead of just touching the Frisbee to the gate as she did when told "Frisbee fetch gate."

Ake showed her ability to grasp a new concept when taught the word "in." During training for the meaning of the word, she was merely instructed "in." She could then choose one object and put it either inside or on top of another for a correct response. The first time she was given a sentence using "in"—"basket hoop in"—she correctly and without hesitation picked up the hoop and placed it in the basket.

Both animals also responded appropriately when asked to carry out an action on an object that wasn't in the tank. If asked "ball fetch," for example, when no ball was in the tank, the dolphin would search for a ball, then return to its station without fetching any object. This reaction led the scientists to start another set of experiments that required the animals to report the absence of items. A paddle representing the word "no" was put in the tank. Ake was taught to press the paddle when a trainer pointed at it. Then she was given a sentence in which the object asked for was missing from the tank. When she returned to her station, the trainer pointed at the paddle. She pressed it and was given her fish reward. She immediately understood that the paddle stood for "no, that object isn't here," and from then on used it to report the absence of a requested item.

DOLPHINS AND KIDS

How do dolphins stack up against young humans in their understanding of syntax? This is not an easy comparison to make, but there are some studies of how well children interpret sentences at different ages. If given toys or puppets and asked to act out a sentence such as "The butterfly chased the dog," young children tend to pay more attention to what seems possible to them than to what the sentence actually says. Since the idea of butterflies chasing dogs seems unlikely, they would think the sentence meant the opposite and act out "The dog chased the butterfly" instead. In a number of studies, children under two years of age could not understand the significance of word order in sentences. Three-year-olds were likely to rely more on what made sense to them than on what the sentences actually said. Only by the time an English-speaking child reaches about five years of age does he or she understand syntax well enough to interpret reversible sentences correctly.

Experiments with Japanese children back up these results. In Japanese, the verb comes last in a sentence, preceded by the other sentence elements. The direct object and indirect object have endings added that indicate which is which. Either one can appear first or second in the sentence. Japanese children were given a choice of two toys and told to move one (the direct object) to the other (the indirect object). Since only the two named toys were present, children would be correct 50 percent of the time by chance. The youngest children tested—between twenty-seven and thirty-seven months old—were right only 53 percent of the time—essentially no better than chance. Older children did better; curiously, those aged thirty-seven to fifty-four months were correct 82 percent of the time, while the oldest ones, from five years to five years and seven months old, scored only 71 percent correct. The dolphins scored comparably to the children on this type of task, even though they had more items to choose from. Phoenix was right 88 percent of the time when given three-word sentences, and Ake scored 60 percent. For the dolphins, chance choosing would make them right only 4 percent of the time.

LANGUAGE IN THE SEA

While it is interesting to try to compare dolphins with children on this sort of task, it may not mean much. While the dolphins were carefully taught their languages step by step, with special attention paid to the importance of syntax, the children weren't. They had just learned language in the normal human way, by being around people who spoke the language. No one had told them how their languages were put together; they were just learning by example. The comparison does, however, give perspective on some of the difficulties imbedded in language learning. We take our language knowledge for granted. Our memories don't extend back to the time we were struggling to figure out what others were saying and how they were saying it. We feel as if we've always known how to speak our native tongue.

SURPRISING SEA LIONS

While dolphins are generally thought to be especially intelligent animals, sea lions haven't been. They are quite trainable—the "trained seal" balancing a ball on its nose is almost always a sea lion, not a seal—but their brains are significantly smaller for their size than those of dolphins. Could a less bright animal like a sea lion also learn to understand a gestural language? Ronald Schusterman, a psychologist working at the Long Marine Laboratory of the University of California, Santa Cruz, decided to find out. He has worked in somewhat different ways with four California sea lions—Bucky, Rocky, Gertie, and Rio. Rocky's language is very similar to Ake's gestural language. Some details are different—the modifiers refer to color (black and white) and size (large and small, for example). But the construction of the "sentences" is basically the same.

Rocky has done very well. Within about two-and-a-half years, she learned the signs for eleven objects, five modifiers (size and color), and six actions. The "sentences" she is asked to comprehend can have as many as seven different signs—for example, "large white ball—small black football fetch." Thousands of different sentences are possible in Rocky's language.

Rocky is very attentive while at work. She waits by the foot of the signaler before the command is given. At the signs that modify the first object, she turns her head and her eyes sweep the pool. She then looks back to the signaler. When the object is named, she searches more intently, lifting her body partially out of the water, craning her neck to find it. Once she's spotted the object, she swings back to face the signaler again. When the action sign is given, she heads right out and performs the appropriate action most of the time—touching it with her flipper, her tail, or her open mouth, for example—then heads back to get her fish reward.

Like Ake, however, Rocky has trouble remembering where to take an object when she is asked to fetch one item and take it to another. Schusterman and his colleague, Robert Gisiner, carefully analyzed Rocky's performance on these test items. They found that a number of factors affected her success. For example, the more items in the pool when she had to keep two in mind, the worse Rocky's scores were. When she was required to choose only one object, however, her performance was not affected by the number of items in the pool. The researchers came to the conclusion that Rocky couldn't remember the first object signed when a second one was given, even though she had looked about the pool for it and noted where it was. It seemed that learning the second item had knocked the first one out of her memory.

Both Rocky and the dolphin Ake had better results when the object to which another item should be brought— the "goal item"—was one that didn't move, such as a hose pouring water into the tank or a person sitting at the edge of the pool. Rocky, for example, was right only about 40 percent of the time when the goal item could be moved, whereas she made the correct response 70 percent to almost 80 percent of the time when it was fixed in position. Can the animals remember the stationary objects better or is it just that they are more likely to choose such an object at random when they have forgotten the goal item signed? Schusterman came to the conclusion that the second object knocked the first one out of memory and that Rocky's success with stationary objects, and maybe Ake's as well, was due to the preference for stationary objects. Perhaps stationary goal items are easier to remember since they can only function in that way, while transportable objects sometimes are carried and other times function as goal items.

DO DOLPHINS AND SEA LIONS UNDERSTAND "LANGUAGE"?

Louis Herman designed his experiments to bring scientific objectivity to the study of animal language abilities. He hoped in this way to make the results of such work more easy to interpret. But it hasn't worked out that way. Herman feels that his dolphins show at least the beginnings of language capability. First of all, both animals understood the meaning of word order in their own languages. To Herman, this ability indicated an understanding of syntax. Secondly, since both dolphins could correctly carry out sentences they'd never encountered before, Herman felt they showed some general understanding of language.

The psychologist David Premack, who has worked with chimpanzees, however, believes that Herman's work has nothing to do with language. He feels that Herman's dolphins learned two rules. Rule 1 told them to carry out an action on an object; Rule 2 told them to carry out an action with one object upon another. "Surface ball spit" would be an example of Rule 1. "Surface ball fetch bottom Frisbee" would indicate Rule 2. Premack feels that these are really very simple rules that have nothing to do with language. To him, language involves an understanding of the concepts "word" and "sentence."

Schusterman and Gisiner believe that the truth lies somewhere between these two views. By seeing how Rocky responded to nonsense sequences of words, they showed that she had a good grasp of how the words were strung together to make meaning. For example, if Rocky was given the command "ball large fetch" instead of "large ball fetch," she wouldn't even leave her station. If told "person, disc mouth," Rocky would ignore the "person" signal and touch the disc with her mouth. Ake responded in a similar fashion to such commands.

Schusterman and Gisiner agree that the animals' understanding of the "word order" can be described by Premack's two rules. The syntax of the dolphins' languages was based purely on word order. It was a very simple language. In human languages, however, two sentences with different word order can have the same meaning. "The dog chased the cat" and "The cat was chased by the dog" mean the same thing. Schusterman and Gisiner think the dolphins and sea lions associate the word symbol with the object or action it represents as an image rather than as a symbol, a "word."

They believe, however, that this sort of ability represents the beginnings of language, if not language itself. The ability to associate objects and actions with the symbol representing them is essential to language, they feel, even if more sophisticated mental abilities may be required for true language mastery. To them, what the dolphins and sea lions learned was a very simple language that has three categories of signs—object, action, and modifier. These three categories, using Premack's two rules, can be combined into a great variety of sentences.

Obviously, more experiments still need to be done to explore how much animals can grasp of language. Perhaps a way could be found to indicate the role of a word in a sentence using something besides word order—something equivalent to the endings added to words in so many human languages. If animals could understand that kind of artificial language, it would indicate a greater capacity to grasp syntax.

Producing language is more difficult than understanding it. Louis Herman and his coworkers are developing a system that would allow dolphins to produce language using an underwater panel with symbols on it. The dolphins would be able to create sentences by nosing the symbols. The results of these experiments could prove to be very exciting.

Peter is fascinated by the alphabet before he is two years old. Human children have a drive to learn language. Is our striking language ability part of what sets us apart from other animals? How does language promote human culture and aid us in thinking?

—PHOTO BY DOROTHY H. PATENT

9

UNDERSTANDING
ANIMALS

We will never know just what goes on inside animals' heads, but we are beginning to get a glimpse of their mental capabilities. For most of the century, research emphasized the details of learning, using only a few species such as rats and pigeons. But now scientists are becoming increasingly interested in other aspects of animal intelligence such as memory and the ways in which animals use their problem-solving abilities in nature. This is an exciting time, and increasing numbers of researchers are tackling the difficult task of learning how animals think.

FINDING OUT ABOUT ANIMAL MINDS

As the ape language controversy shows, finding ways to use objective methods while studying animal intelligence isn't easy. When humans interact closely with their subjects, objectivity can be lost. But intelligent behavior isn't often used in isolation from stimulating interactive environments. The animal must be motivated to cooperate and to work or the studies will get nowhere. As we learned earlier, Alex the grey parrot has shown some remarkably intelligent behavior. But in order to keep Alex interested in the work, Pepperberg needs to make several concessions to his emotional needs. Alex will only work, for example, when she is in the room. So she sits in a corner where she can't see the objects Alex is presented with. That way, she can't cue him in an unconscious way, and she can function as the "blind" observer who evaluates his responses.

Finding the appropriate training techniques and reward system is critical to research success. Not only did Pepperberg have to modify the techniques of others to teach Alex to talk, but she also had to figure out what reward would work with him. Others before her had tried food rewards and failed to get their birds to learn to use vocalizations as words. Her understanding of the curiosity of the parrot—that getting him to examine and play with an object could be a powerful reward—is one key to Pepperberg's success with Alex.

Alex also gets bored easily and sometimes doesn't want to work. This was a problem until he was taught to say "no" when he wanted a time-out. Now he gets his breaks when he needs them. It has been especially tricky to get Alex to cooperate in the "counting" experiments. Alex's reward is being allowed to manipulate the object he chooses. He gets no special benefit from naming three or five objects, since he can play with only one. It may also be that figuring out numbers is difficult for him. In any case, getting Alex's cooperation with these experiments isn't easy. Instead of answering the question "How many?" Alex might ignore it and say instead, "I want popcorn," or "You tickle me?"

Avoiding boredom is one of the trickiest tasks when working with intelligent animals, just as it is with humans. Going over and over the same sorts of questions and problems is no more fun for them than it is for us. Yet reproducibility is an important criterion of science. Pepperberg does her best to get around this problem with Alex by letting him take breaks when he wants and by mixing up the sorts of problems presented to him. Only one or two quantity problems are included in each working session so that he won't balk. It takes considerable ingenuity and patience to find ways to get such creatures to continue to cooperate.

AS NATURAL AS POSSIBLE

Pepperberg used the natural behavior of grey parrots when she chose her training method for Alex. She took advantage of the dueting behavior of pairs to key into a built-in learning mechanism, and she succeeded where others have failed. Alan Kamil and his associates experimented directly with the caching behavior of the Clark's nutcracker, modifying the environment to make scientific evaluation of the bird's memory possible. If they had tried to get the bird to remember something different, such as a sequence of colored squares, the results might have been unimpressive. They may also have failed if they had expected the bird to hide objects other than its natural food.

Keeping the situation natural enough so that the animals can show off their abilities while maintaining scientific rigor is a tricky balancing act. Seyfarth and Cheney, in their studies of vervet monkeys, were able to succeed in the wild by playing back recordings or by modifying the environment—for example, placing a gazelle carcass in a nearby tree—and then observing the animals' responses. Using their work as a model, perhaps other scientists will be able to probe the intricacies of how animals use their brains in nature.

Since so much of what we call intelligence shows itself in a social context, studies in nature are especially important. An artificial colony of, say, monkeys in the laboratory is no substitute for the natural groupings found in the wild. The wild group has developed over time, influenced by births and deaths, with social status closely tied to biological relationships and acquaintance spanning the time from birth to death. A laboratory colony, however, may consist of animals that haven't known one another since infancy, brought together from different regions. They are kept in a small area, with no room for escape from the intensity of social interactions, so that normal behavior may be modified or exaggerated. For example, wolves in the wild range over areas of many square miles. They have lots of breathing room. Captive packs, even in an enclosure of several acres, are very restricted and may show much more frequent social interactions than wild packs, probably because of their small range. The lowest ranking animal also has no way to escape, and unnatural violence can result from this inability to run away.

By studying animals in their natural environment, scientists can explore the aspects of intelligence that are important to the animals themselves. How does this behavior help them survive over time? What aspects of intelligent behavior have been developed in a particular species to allow it to be successful? The caching behavior of nutcrackers and other birds, for example, requires the evolution of a finely tuned, very impressive memory capability beyond that of creatures considered in other ways as more "intelligent."

Life in the wild is difficult. Wild animals don't have grocery stores where they can buy food. They can't wear a heavy coat or retreat indoors when bad weather threatens. Most live in a constant state of alertness as well, for almost all of them are the food that keeps other animals alive. When investigations of animals' mental capabilities were restricted to laboratory learning by rats, pigeons, and a few monkeys, scientists were not terribly impressed by the results. But nowadays, with more attention being paid to their natural behavior, animals are coming across as more mentally talented than laboratory scientists ever thought possible.

Chimpanzees are especially intelligent, yet the world met Jane Goodall's revelations about chimp tool manufacture and use with amazement. Now we know that not only chimps but also monkeys can make and use tools and that some birds such as blue jays can learn to use sticks as tools, if not to shape them for that purpose. It seems that the more we look, the more we find, and that we have been grossly underestimating animal mental abilities for a long time. Even honeybees, with their sophisticated preprogrammed behavior, have room in their tiny brains for special and remarkable types of learning.

WHAT WE KNOW NOW

Since both laboratory studies such as those of Pepperberg with Alex and field studies such as Seyfarth and Cheney's on vervet monkeys are revealing that animals are capable of far more mentally than we ever before suspected, we must be certain that we use a broad definition of intelligence. That way, we have the best chance of finding out as much as possible about how animals use their brains.

We are learning how the details of what animals do and don't learn are related to their differing life styles. Sea birds provide perhaps the best example here. Gulls and terns are related kinds of sea birds that nest in colonies along the shore and on islands. What they learn about their nests and chicks relates directly to their nesting habits. Royal terns, for example, nest in a densely packed colony where identifying individual nests is very difficult. These birds lay eggs that vary greatly in appearance, and the adults learn to recognize their own eggs in the mass confusion of the colony. Herring gulls, on the other hand, space their nests farther apart. They can recognize their nests, but they cannot identify their own eggs. When herring gull chicks are very young, they stay in the nest, and the adults cannot tell one chick from another. By the time the chicks are older, however, and wander from the nest, the parents can identify them individually and continue to take care of them. The kittiwake, a kind of tern, nests along steep cliffs, so the chicks can't leave home. These birds memorize the location of their nests, but they can't recognize their own eggs or chicks.

While not being able to recognize their own offspring may seem strange to us, for the kittiwake it makes perfect sense. There is no need biologically for the bird to be able to identify its chicks since they never stray from one spot. And we don't know if these different bird species might be capable of learning more than they do in nature. For example, we don't know if herring gulls could recognize their own eggs if they varied in appearance as much as those of royal terns; no one has tested this idea.

While some aspects of life, such as the fact that a kittiwake's chick can't leave its nest, are quite predictable, life in the wild is full of variability and unpredictability. The interactions of organisms with the environment are so complex that rarely can behavior be fully programmed in advance. The honeybee's food supply may come from yellow buttercups one day and white daisies soon thereafter, and the wolf must be ready to react quickly to its prey's unpredictable behavior.

Animals are prepared for variability in their environment, and it shows in laboratory experiments. Take, for example, a pigeon trained to peck at an orange key to get food. When the bird is presented with keys of other colors, it will also peck at them in proportion to their relationship to orange. It will try out a yellow key more often than a blue one. If it gets nothing when it pecks at yellow, soon it will stop trying. Not only that, but not being rewarded for yellow will dampen the bird's enthusiasm somewhat for orange. But if the bird consistently is rewarded for pecking only at the orange key, the result will be that it narrows the range of colors it tries.

The pigeon's behavior shows a constant tendency to be ready to adapt to changing circumstances. It doesn't get "stuck on" responding to only one color. While its rewards in the laboratory may be quite predictable, the factors associated with a good food source in the wild are more likely to vary with time.

Because of nature's variability, thinking can come in very handy for animals. It allows them to adapt to changing circumstances. But thinking has its costs, as it involves the necessity of learning first. The life of solitary wasps is so short that they don't have time to learn the fine points of how to dig nests or evaluate the needs of their young. They have to know these things right from the start, so the behavior must be patterned into the genes.

The environment changes over time, too. An animal that lives longer, therefore, is likely to encounter greater variability in its surroundings than one with a short life span. Insects that live only a few days as adults don't need to be able to learn much. Some of them don't even feed. Their only concern is mating and laying eggs before they are eaten or die naturally.

If we keep these thoughts in mind, it makes sense that the animals known to be the most intelligent are often those that live the longest. Parrots and jays are especially long-lived birds. Dolphins can live for thirty-five years or more, and elephants may survive until sixty or older. Such animals also tend to have few offspring, for the youngsters need to be protected and cared for while they learn what they need to know to survive.

GENERAL RULES

Despite the differences in the details of what and how animals learn, there is also a very important basic principle behind most learning. In our world, causality and connectedness are everywhere. One event causes another or is associated with it in some way. If one yellow flower in a patch contains nectar, the others probably also will. If the sky gets dark with clouds, rain is likely to follow. If a lion crouches in the grass nearby, she is probably about to rush out to capture prey.

The importance of being able to link one event or sign to another one of significance is so great that associational learning—the ability to associate one thing with another—appears to be found in all animals that have been tested. The research carried out by behaviorists for so many years was basically testing variations on the ability of animals to associate different stimuli with reward or punishment.

The quickness of animals to make associations can get in the way when scientists test animal intelligence. Clever Hans was so good at associating the unconscious activities of the humans watching him that he knew when to stop pawing his hoof. Researchers must design their experiments to avoid this problem. Rocky and other sea lions seem to look for clues that will make their work more predictable. If the "sentences" they are given aren't arranged in truly random fashion, the animals may jump to conclusions about what to expect and be led astray. In nature, making associations has the advantage of allowing an animal to guess about the future, letting it stay one step ahead.

Because all vertebrate animals tested in the laboratory can successfully make associations, a British psychologist, Euan MacPhail, has made the daring statement that there are no differences in intelligence among vertebrates other than humans! Unfortunately, MacPhail never defines just what he means by intelligence; he relies on common understanding. But his understanding doesn't necessarily agree with that of others. He would, for example, not count the extraordinary memory capacity of the Clark's nutcracker as a part of general intelligence but rather as a special ability. The only capacity he includes in intelligence other than associational learning is language capability, which he reserves for humans.

MacPhail's emphasis on associational learning as the key element of intelligence is important. But if all animals really were identically intelligent, there would be no point in studying their mental abilities at all. Extensive research on animals other than rats and pigeons is so recent and comparatively limited—no one has worked with kangaroos, deer, cows, snakes, or salamanders, for example—that such a bold statement is really premature. And even most of the work with those two laboratory standbys has been very limited in what it actually tests.

DIFFERENCES IN MINDS
Associational learning may be such an important and pervasive aspect of intelligent behavior that all animals can

accomplish it, but that doesn't mean there aren't important differences in the mechanisms of such learning in different kinds of animals. Behaviorists once thought that an animal had to go through the actual motor patterns of behavior before being able to learn. We now know that a rat can learn the pattern of a maze while being carried through it by a human and that a chimp can remember where food or danger is located when it is transported by a person.

But we've also found out that honeybees don't remember the location of food sources unless they actually fly back themselves from the food to the hive and that they only learn the color of the flower as they are landing. With bees, learning and memory can be keyed in very closely with the normal sequences of motor behavior. Even though the bee can learn and communicate an amazing amount of information for such a tiny creature, its learning is largely tied to a more mechanical, computer-like nervous system than that of mammals like rats or chimps.

The special abilities of some creatures such as songbirds also show that animal minds aren't identical. When the young male bird is learning the songs of his species, he can recognize the appropriate notes and patterns even when he hears many different birds singing. Months later, when he himself is old enough to establish his territory and proclaim it to others of his kind, he will sing the right way. We haven't recognized this type of learning in other animals.

Even within the same species there can be significant differences in important aspects of song learning. Donald Kroodsma and Jared Verner of the Forest Service in Fresno found that eastern marsh wrens learn far fewer songs than western marsh wrens. An adult eastern bird knows thirty to sixty songs while a western one can sing as many as 220. Even when raised under identical conditions in the laboratory, the eastern birds learned no more than sixty-four songs while western ones memorized as many as 113. In western birds, the part of the brain controlling song is larger than in the eastern wrens, so the difference can even be correlated with the brain. The ecology of the two subspecies is different in ways that could be associated with the songs, too. The western birds live in more dense populations than eastern ones and stay in the same area year around instead of migrating, so they probably interact with one another more. More interaction may require more complex communication.

Associational learning may be the basis of intelligence, but animals clearly need mental talents keyed to how they live. The nutcracker needs an enormous memory, while the bee must know the color and location of the flowers currently providing nectar. Humans have other needs. Just because bees and nutcrackers can't speak and write doesn't mean they aren't intelligent—each animal is the most capable and the best adapted to living in its appointed environment. We don't say that humans aren't intelligent because they can't memorize where nuts are hidden or tell which gull chick belongs to which parents.

WHAT MAKES US DIFFERENT?
If animals think, if they are aware, they are more like us than we once considered them to be. The consequences to human thinking of animal intelligence are profound. One

reason for human resistance to the idea of intelligent animals seems to be a need to maintain a distance from other living things. People want to feel superior, especially when it comes to intelligence, for we feel that our minds are a significant part of what makes us "special." Thus, the idea of thinking animals makes many people uncomfortable. If we can't see ourselves as superior, our place in the universe seems less special.

Other people, however, see the issue in a completely different light. They realize that, if animals can think, they are more akin to us. If we are more alike, we are more wholly a part of the universe, more integrated within it. For these people, the idea of being able to tap into animal minds and perhaps communicate with them is exciting. Maybe we can learn important things from the animals. Perhaps we can feel more attuned to our own true nature by learning about and respecting the other forms of life on our planet.

If animals can reason, use tools, recognize quantity, and perhaps comprehend syntax, what makes us different? Clearly we are different. No animal has discovered mathematical principles, written a book, painted a portrait, produced a symphony, or traveled to the moon. Why do we appear so mentally superior to our animal cousins?

Animals live very much in the moment and the very near future. Where the next meal will come from is probably as far ahead as animals think. The future-oriented activities of animals tend to be instinctive rather than thoughtful. While the memory of a Clark's nutcracker for its food caches is very impressive, the caching of the food itself is an inborn trait; the bird knows about it without having to learn. This tendency shows even in mammals. Bears develop huge appetites in the fall and put on fat that feeds them through the winter. They don't think ahead to the time of denning; they are just very hungry. Even for humans, projecting into the future is hard.

Although it is difficult, people can think beyond the next meal. Perhaps language is the key that allows us to think beyond the present, concrete reality, to imagine tomorrow and the consequences of what we do today. The animal languages we know about and the artificial languages we have used with apes, dolphins, and sea lions are all communication systems, nothing more. They apply specific symbols—words or signs—to specific objects, properties of objects such as size or color, and actions, such as fetch. But the meanings of the words or signs do not go beyond these concrete associations.

Words are much more full of meaning for humans. The word "word" itself has a dizzying array of connotations that go far beyond spoken syllables. Its meanings extend from an arrangement of letters on a page or the spoken syllables all the way to the word with a capital "W," meaning the Bible. I can promise you something by giving you "my word," or you can get into trouble because of "the word of the law."

Human language is a symbolic system as well as a straight communication system. The hungry pigeon pecks when it sees red; it knows red means food. But when we hear the word "red" or see it in print, a variety of symbolic meanings may flash through our minds. If we call someone a "red," we are labeling that person as a communist. If I say, "Boy, was my face red!" you know I felt very embarrassed about something. If we comment that someone "saw red," we know he was very angry. Ask someone what the word "red" brings to mind—you'll get many answers including possibly blood, sunsets, communist, embarrassment, anger, warning, and so forth. Thus, language allows us to use our minds to go far beyond immediate reality.

LANGUAGE AND THINKING

Language also streamlines thinking. Words, with their symbolic and concrete meanings, are aids to thought. When we think, we use our language to help us find our way and to organize our ideas. Language helps us file things away in our memory and organize ideas and information mentally. Even the limited amount of mental organization imposed by ASL training on chimpanzees may have allowed them to think in more organized ways. Apes that learned ASL scored better on problem-solving tasks than did apes without such training.

Language helps us construct our view of reality. We use it to visualize the world and to think about it. When we employ language to communicate our ideas to one another, our use of words shapes our ideas as much as the ideas shape the way we use words. For this reason, different languages help impose different world views, and some languages are better for some types of thought expression than others. English, for example, is a useful language for scientific communication. The grammatical structure is quite unambiguous, and the words can be clearly defined. Chinese, on the other hand, is not as easily adapted to science; it is better for the communication of philosophical ideas. Traditional Chinese uses characters rather than letters in its written form. The letters of our alphabet carry no particular history or emotional tone with them. Chinese characters, on the other hand, don't just represent sounds. They also have a literary history that may go with them when they are used. An educated person writing in Chinese may purposely employ that history to get across the emotional tone or complexities of the subject matter. While this depth of meaning can make Chinese a great language for the communication of ideas, the "history" attached to the characters can get in the way of communicating pure fact that is meant to be devoid of underlying meaning.

Language has another important function as well—it allows the accumulation of information over generations. Animals can learn from one another, like the Japanese macaques washing sweet potatoes and the Gombe chimpanzees learning how to make and use termite catchers. But the degree to which language allows humans to pass down culture and knowledge through generations far surpasses what animals learn from one another. In cultures with written languages, people can even learn things their living elders know nothing about, an advantage not available to the animals.

WHAT IS A HUMAN?
Studies of animal intelligence have only scratched the surface, and many fascinating facts still await us. How much will parrots like Alex be able to understand with continued training? Can apes develop a "society" in which symbolic rewards—money—are earned and spent, indicating that

they have an ability to plan beyond the immediate future? Will dolphin language ever be unraveled and, if so, will it prove to be more complex than the natural forms of communication used by other animals?

These questions and more all speak to the importance of further research. Not only is it interesting to learn about our animal neighbors on this planet, but studying them tells us things about ourselves, about what makes us like them and what makes us different. At this point, we can say that our highly developed language skills allow us to project ourselves into the future so we can plan far ahead. Our undeveloped bodies require many tools to allow us to exploit our environment, and our lack of specialization combines with our problem-solving abilities to enable us to live in almost every environment available on earth. Our ability to use the knowledge we acquire through experience to help us solve problems appears vastly to exceed that of other creatures. But their talents are also impressive and go far beyond what was assumed not so many years ago.

SOURCES FOR QUOTATIONS

p. 11: Griffin, Donald R., *Animal Thinking*, Harvard University Press, Cambridge, MA, 1984, p. 111.

p. 61: (1) *The New York Times Magazine*, May 24, 1982, p. 48; (2) *Self Magazine*, March, 1982, p. 63; (3) *Cognition*, Glass, A. L., Holyoak, K. J., and Santa, J. L., Addison Wesley, 1979, p. 326.

p. 66–67: Pepperberg, Irene, "Functional vocalizations by an African Grey Parrot *(Psittacus erithacus),*" *Zeitschrift für Tierpsychologie* 55:139–60, 1981, p. 142.

p. 71: Pepperberg, Irene, "Evidence for Conceptual Quantitative Abilities in the African Grey Parrot: Labeling of Cardinal Sets," *Ethology* 75:37–61, 1987, p. 52–53.

p. 111: Gardner, B. T., and Gardner, R. A., "Comparing the early utterances of child and chimpanzee," In *Minnesota Symposium on Child Psychology* (ed. A. Pick), vol. 8:3–23, 1974, p. 20.

p. 112: Fouts, Roger, "Capacities for language in great apes," in *Society and Psychology of Primates* (ed. R. H. Tuttle), Mouton, The Hague, 1975, pp. 371–90; quote on p. 385.

p. 112–113: ibid., p. 387.

p. 115: Fouts, R., M. Hannum, C. O'Sullivan, and K. Schneider, "Chimpanzee Conversations," in *Language Development* (ed. J. Kuzo), Erlbaum, Hillsdale, N.J., 1982.

p. 116–117: Linden, Eugene, *Silent Partners*, Times Books, New York, 1986, p. 121.

GLOSSARY

ASL: American Sign Language, used by the deaf, a modified version of which has been taught to apes.

ASSOCIATIVE LEARNING: Learning that associates a stimulus with an expected outcome.

BEHAVIORISM: The theory that animals learn by remembering patterns resulting in rewards or avoidance of punishment.

CLASSICAL CONDITIONING: The process by which an animal learns to associate a stimulus, such as a bell ringing, with a reward, such as food.

CLEVER HANS PHENOMENON: An animal response provoked when the animal notices subtle, unintended cues given by humans present.

COGNITION: A word for thinking that avoids the connotation of consciousness.

ENCEPHALIZATION: The development of a large concentration of nervous tissue in the head—in other words, a brain.

ENCEPHALIZATION QUOTIENT: A measure of relative brain size that takes body size into account.

ETHOLOGY: The study of the natural behavior of animals.

EXTINCTION: "Unlearning"—the process by which animals learn that a particular behavior no longer brings a reward.

GANGLIA: Clusters of nerve cells that send out nerves to parts of the body.

HABITUATION: The process by which an animal learns to ignore a stimulus that has no positive or negative consequences.

IMPRINTING: Learning that occurs only during a brief critical period of a young animal's life, in which it associates a particular object with a particular function—such as learning to follow its mother.

INSTINCT: An inborn pattern of behavior.

LINGUISTIC COMMUNICATION: Communication that uses words and syntax that have been learned rather than instinctive signals.

STIMULUS-RESPONSE LEARNING (S-R LEARNING): A term including the kinds of conditioning experiments behaviorists believe can explain all learned behavior.

SYNTAX: The internal structure—grammar—of a language.

TEMPLATE: An imprecise pattern, present in an animal's brain, which an animal tries to match with its behavior.

RESEARCH SOURCES

In writing this book I used a wide variety of resources, including the following books, most of which were symposia with many authors. I also read many articles in scientific journals, including *Zeitschrift für Tierpsychologie* (Frank and Pepperberg), *Behavioral and Brain Sciences* (MacPhail), *Animal Learning & Behavior* (Pepperberg), *Journal of Comparative Psychology* (Herman and Westergaard), *Neuroscience & Biobehavioral Reviews* (Herman), *Psychological Record* (Schusterman), *Proceedings of the National Academy of Science* (Kroodsma et al.), *Animal Behavior* (Kamil), and *Journal of Experimental Psychology* (Kamil).

Greenberg, Gary, and Ethel Tobach, editors. *Cognition, Language, and Consciousness: Integrative Levels.* Erlbaum, Hillsdale, N.J., 1987.

Griffin, D. R., editor. *Animal Mind—Human Mind*. Springer-Verlag, Berlin, 1982.

Jerison, H. J., and I. Jerison. *Intelligence and Evolutionary Biology*. Springer-Verlag, Berlin, 1988.

Lieberman, Philip. *The Biology and Evolution of Language*. Harvard University Press, Cambridge, Mass., 1984.

Marler, P., and H. S. Terrace, editors. *The Biology of Learning*. Springer-Verlag, Berlin, 1984.

Masterton, R. B., et al., editors. *Evolution of Brain and Behavior in Vertebrates* (2 volumes). Erlbaum, Hillsdale, N.J., 1976.

Premack, David. *Gavagai! Or the Future History of the Animal Language Controversy*. MIT Press, Cambridge, Mass., 1986.

Roitblat, H. L., T. G. Bever, and H. S. Terrace, editors. *Animal Cognition*, Erlbaum, Hillsdale, N.J., 1984.

Schusterman, Ronald J., Jeanette A. Thomas, and Forrest G. Wood, editors. *Dolphin Cognition and Behavior: A Comparative Approach*. Erlbaum, Hillsdale, N.J., 1986.

Sebeok, Thomas A., and Robert Rosenthal, editors. *The Clever Hans Phenomenon: Communication with Horses, Whales, Apes, and People*. New York Academy of Sciences, New York, 1981 (Annals, volume 364).

Smuts, Barbara B., et al, editors. *Primate Societies*. University of Chicago Press, Chicago, 1986.

Tuttle, R. H., editor. *Socioecology and Psychology of Primates*. Mouton, The Hague, 1975.

Weiskrantz, L., editor. *Animal Intelligence*. Philosophical Transactions of the Royal Society of London, Volume 308, February, 1985.

SUGGESTED READING

BOOKS

Ferry, Georgina, editor. *The Understanding of Animals*. Basil Blackwell & New Scientist, Oxford, England, 1984. A collection of articles from the British magazine *New Scientist*, many of which deal with animal intelligence.

Griffin, Donald R. *Animal Thinking*. Harvard University Press, Cambridge, Mass., 1984. A book for scientists and intelligent nonspecialists alike, full of interesting ideas.

Hoage, R. J., and Larry Goldman, editors. *Animal Intelligence*. Smithsonian Institution Press, Washington, D.C., 1986. A collection of articles written by scientists; sometimes difficult for a nonscientist but well written and very interesting.

Linden, Eugene. *Silent Partners—The Legacy of the Ape Language Ex-

periments. Times Books (Random House), New York, 1986. A very readable book discussing the history and fate of the ape language experiments.

Mortenson, Joseph. *Whale Songs and Wasp Maps: The Mystery of Animal Thinking*. Dutton, New York, 1987. Includes history of ideas on animal thinking and much material on consciousness.

Pryor, Karen. *Lads before the Wind—Adventures in Porpoise Training*. Harper and Row, New York, 1975. A very interesting book by an animal trainer, with many anecdotes indicating the intelligence of dolphins.

MAGAZINE ARTICLES

Abrahamson, David. "Do Animals Think?" *National Wildlife*, August/September, 1983.

Cowley, Geoffrey. "The Wisdom of Animals." *Newsweek*, May 23, 1988. A good survey of research on animal intelligence, with photos.

Davidson, Keay, and Janet L. Hopson, "Gorilla Business," *Image*, April 10, 1988. Discusses Koko and whether what is done with her qualifies as science.

Ehmann, James. "The Elephant as Artist." *National Wildlife*, February/March, 1987. Covers a topic not discussed in this book—are there animal artists? If so, what does this say about intelligence and consciousness?

Fox, Michael W. "Animals Can't Think? Think Again." *McCall's*, March, 1984. An article by a scientist who studies dogs and their relatives.

Horgan, John. "Do Bees Think? The Discoverer of Bat 'Sonar' Thinks about Animals' Thoughts." *Scientific American*, May, 1989. An article about Donald Griffin and his concepts of animal thinking.

Gould, James L. "Do Honeybees Know What They Are Doing?" *Natural History*, June/July, 1979. A discussion of learning and instinct in honeybees, written by a scientist who has done much of the research.

Gould, James L., and Peter Marler. "Learning by Instinct." *Scientific American*, January, 1987. Two prominent scientists—one studies bees, the other, birds—team up to discuss the interactions of learning and instinct.

SUGGESTED READING

Gould, Stephen Jay. "Evolution and the Brain." *Natural History*, January, 1975. A discussion of Jerison's ideas on intelligence and brain size.

Jolly, Alison. "A New Science That Sees Animals as Conscious Beings." *Smithsonian*, March, 1985. About Donald Griffin and his work.

Lewis, Jacquie. "Alex, the Intellectual Grey." *Bird Talk*, October, 1989. A discussion of Irene Pepperberg's work with Alex, with photos.

Linden, Eugene. "Suburban Chimp." *Omni*, May, 1986. About a chimp that lives with people and the implications for animal intelligence.

Rose, Kenneth Jon. "How Animals Think." *Science Digest*, February, 1984. A general discussion of animal thinking.

Starr, Douglas, "This Bird Has a Way with Words," *National Wildlife*, February/March, 1988. A visit with Irene Pepperberg and Alex, discussing what Alex can do.

INDEX

INDEX

INDEX

ALSO BY DOROTHY HINSHAW PATENT

(continued on next page)